BUILDING L.E.G.A.C.Y.™

THE FRAMEWORK TO INSPIRE AND EMPOWER

DR. SHATOYA BLACK

EDITED BY
NICOLE QUEEN

All rights reserved. Published in the United States by Vision Publishing House, LLC.

Vision Publishing House
support@vision-publishinghouse.com
www.vision-publishinghouse.com

ISBN: 978-1-955297-81-3
LCCN: 2025900222

This book is established to provide information and inspiration to all readers. It is designed with the understanding that the author is not engaged to render any psychological, legal, or any other kind of professional advice. The content is the sole expression of the author. All events, locales, and conversations have been recreated based on the author's memory. And to maintain anonymity, some names have purposely been excluded. In addition, some identifying details have been left out to protect the privacy of specific individuals and the integrity of the author's experiences with them. The author is not liable for any physical, psychological, emotional, financial, or commercial damages, including, but not limited to special, incidental, consequential, or other damages. All readers are responsible for their own choices, actions, and results.

To the dreamers and doers, the leaders and learners— may your journey be guided by purpose, resilience, and the belief that your impact transforms generations

"Do the best you can until you know better. Then when you know better you do better."

"If you are going to live, leave a legacy. Make a mark on the world that can not be erased."

— MAYA ANGELOU

CONTENTS

Introduction   ix

1. LEADERSHIP   I
   Discovering Your Leadership Style   I
   Choosing the Right Leadership Style   4
   Self-Leadership   5
   The Weight of Leadership: Barriers & Lessons   9
   Legacy Leadership: Creating a Lasting Impact   11
   Personal Lessons: My Leadership Journey   15
   Leadership Review   17
   Leadership in Action   20
   Leadership Challenge   22

2. EDUCATION   25
   Knowledge as Empowerment   25
   Breaking Barriers Through Education   27
   Lifelong Learning: A Journey Without End   30
   The Transformative Power of Education   33
   Empowering Others Through Education   35
   Personal Application   37
   Education in Action   40
   Education Challenge   41

3. GROWTH   43
   Personal Growth: Resilience in Adversity   43
   Embracing Discomfort for Progress   45
   Critical Transition Points   48
   Growth is a Choice   49
   My Personal Journey   50
   Growth in Action   52
   Growth Challenge   53

4. ADVOCACY   55
   Advocating for Yourself   55
   Advocating for Others   57
   Giving Others a Voice   59

Fighting for Opportunities   60
The Legacy of Advocacy   62
Advocacy in Action   64
Advocacy Challenge   65

5. COMMUNITY   69
The Importance of Having a Community   69
Community Building and Its Effects   71
A Lack of Community and Its Impact   72
Communities Create Opportunities   74
Effects of Mentorship   75
Giving Back Strengthens Your Foundation   77
Communal Strength   78
Community in Action   80
Community Challenge   81

6. YIELDING   85
Faith as the Foundation   86
Letting Go and Trusting the Process   87
A Story of Surrender and Blessings   88
Yielding and Holistic Success   90
Yielding in Action   93
Yielding Challenge   94

7. THE JOURNEY OF L.E.G.A.C.Y.™   97
Live Your L.E.G.A.C.Y.™   99

Additional Resources   101
Acknowledgments   105
About the Author   107

INTRODUCTION

Your legacy isn't something that begins when your story ends; it's a journey of the life you live that starts in the present moment. It's built in the choices you make, the relationships you nurture, and the values you live out daily. The L.E.G.A.C.Y.™ framework is a holistic approach to success and roadmap for building a life of impact, resilience, perseverance, and purpose. It's a framework that empowers you to not only dream of a meaningful life, but to actively create one.

Each pillar of L.E.G.A.C.Y.™ — Leadership, Education, Growth, Advocacy, Community, and Yielding— represents a vital component of living a life that leaves a lasting imprint. These principles aren't just abstract ideas; they are actionable, practical steps that help you align with your purpose and navigate challenges with grace.

Through this framework, you'll discover that your legacy isn't something you leave behind—it's something you live every day. It is a holistic approach to success and practical application that incorporates the lived experiences as vital to inspiring and empowering great outcomes for individuals, organizations, families, programs, and business.

THE MEANING OF L.E.G.A.C.Y.™

The L.E.G.A.C.Y.™ framework was created to guide you in becoming the best version of yourself while positively influencing those around you. It emphasizes that building a legacy doesn't require grand gestures or perfect timing. Instead, it starts with small, intentional actions taken consistently from a holistic perspective. Each letter of the acronym reflects the areas that should be used to shift your mind to a holistic perspective, as it creates a roadmap to determining what a life of success looks like for you. The L.E.G.A.C.Y.™ Framework is timeless and can be used as an assessment at different stages of your life deter-mining needs and the pillars you will focus on to address the needs.

Here's a glimpse into the pillars of L.E.G.A.C.Y.™:

- **Leadership**: Leadership begins with self-leadership. It's about taking ownership of your choices, inspiring others through your actions, and leading with integrity, vision, and a standard of excellence.

- **Education**: Education is a lifelong journey that empowers you to grow, make informed decisions, and align your knowledge with your purpose, goals, and stepping stone plans.

- **Growth**: Growth happens when you step outside your comfort zone and embrace the discomfort that fuels transformation. It's a shift in mindset, and a willingness to change behaviors that affect desired outcomes and objectives.

- **Advocacy**: Advocacy is about speaking up for yourself and others, championing equity, and creating opportunities for those who need them. This area also requires you to be a self-advocate to develop and enhance your identity, as well as gain confidence in elevating your voice.

- **Community**: A thriving community provides connection, support, and collaboration. It reminds us that no one achieves greatness alone. It's important that we not just be in a group of people, but find a community that cares and embraces cultural sensitivity.

- **Yielding**: Yielding is the act of surrendering control, trusting the process, embracing the journey, being teachable, and allowing faith to guide you through uncertainty. Many times, others recognize qualities and abilities in you that push you toward opportunities you never imagined for yourself. It's equally important to understand the significance of timing—some opportunities require you to seize the moment when it presents itself.

These pillars, collectively, form the foundation for a life lived with intention, resilience, and purpose.

IMPLEMENTING THE L.E.G.A.C.Y.™ FRAMEWORK

There's no perfect time to start building your legacy—the time is now. Whether you're stepping into a new chapter of your life or reflecting on the path you've traveled so far, the L.E.G.A.C.Y.™ framework offers practical steps to create impact:

- **Leadership**: Take ownership of one area of your life— whether it's your career, relationships, or personal habits.

Commit to making intentional decisions that reflect your values.

- **Education**: Learn something new that aligns with your goals. Seek out books, courses, conferences, associations, mentors, coach, that can help you grow.

- **Growth**: Challenge yourself to step outside your comfort zone. This might mean pursuing a goal you've been hesitant about or trying something completely new.

- **Advocacy**: Support someone in need, whether through mentorship, encouragement, or speaking up for their rights, even if that person is you.

- **Community**: Build or strengthen a meaningful connection that provides care. Reach out to someone, join a group, or collaborate on a project that aligns with your purpose and goals.

- **Yielding**: Spend intentional time in prayer, meditation, or reflection. Ask for direction, trust the process, and embrace faith in the journey ahead.

LIVING YOUR LEGACY

Your legacy is built in the small, consistent actions you take each day. It's the lives you touch, the values you uphold, and the courage you show in the face of challenges. By embracing the L.E.G.A.C.Y.™ framework, you create a life of meaning, impact, and purpose—one that inspires others to do the same.

You don't have to wait for the perfect moment to begin. The steps you take today shape the story you'll tell tomorrow. So take that first step—your legacy starts now.

As we move forward, each chapter will explore the individual pillars of the L.E.G.A.C.Y.™ framework in depth. Together, we'll break down how Leadership, Education, Growth, Advocacy, Community, and Yielding can be woven into the fabric of your daily life. Each principle will serve as a guide, equipping you with actionable steps, reflective prompts, and the inspiration to live out your legacy with intention and purpose.

Let's navigate this journey together—step by step, pillar by pillar —toward building a life that leaves a lasting imprint.

Your legacy awaits.

GUIDED REFLECTION

Before you turn the pages to begin to integrate the L.E.G.A.C.Y.™ framework into your life, take a moment to reflect:

1. What does your current legacy look like?

_____

_____

_____

_____

_____

_____

_____

_____

_____

_____

2. Which pillar of L.E.G.A.C.Y.™ resonates most with you right now?

_____

_____

_____

_____

_____

_____

_____

_____

_____

_____

3. What small steps can you take today to embody these principles?

_____

_____

_____

_____

_____

_____

_____

_____

_____

_____

_____

_____

_____

_____

_____

_____

4. Who in your life can you support, mentor, or collaborate with to create impact?

_____

_____

_____

_____

_____

_____

_____

_____

_____

_____

_____

_____

_____

_____

_____

_____

5. How can you embrace surrender and trust in the process as you move forward?

_____

_____

_____

_____

_____

_____

_____

_____

_____

_____

_____

As you explore each of the upcoming chapters, revisit your responses to see where you are on your L.E.G.A.C.Y.™ journey. Reflect back on your responses as a guide to assess your progress, celebrate your growth, and identify areas where adjustments might be needed.

Your responses will serve as a living record of your journey, offering clarity and direction as you embrace each pillar of the framework. By staying intentional and reflective, you'll ensure that your legacy continues to evolve, as it aligns with your purpose and goals.

1

LEADERSHIP

L eadership is more than a title or position—it's a mindset, a responsibility, and an opportunity to guide others toward a shared vision. True leadership transcends authority; it is the ability to influence, inspire, and create a lasting impact. While many view leadership as hierarchical, its essence lies in character, empathy, and integrity.

At its core, leadership is about self-awareness and understanding others. It is the balance between making tough decisions and fostering a collaborative environment. As a leader, you are tasked with not only achieving goals, but also leaving a legacy that others can build upon and thrive in. Leadership demands decisiveness, clear communication, adaptability, shared vision, and the ability to foster trust and empowerment.

DISCOVERING YOUR LEADERSHIP STYLE

Leadership is not a one-size-fits-all concept. The way a leader chooses to guide their team often depends on their personality, perspective, values, goals, and the unique challenges they face. Effective leadership involves not only understanding these styles, but also knowing when and how to apply them. Each leadership style offers a distinct approach to decision-making, team management, and achieving results. Let's delve into the most common leadership styles and their defining characteristics:

- Democratic leadership emphasizes collaboration and inclusivity, allowing team members to participate in decision-making. While the leader retains final decision-making authority, this style fosters a sense of ownership and accountability among the team. It thrives in environments where diverse perspectives are valued, creativity is encouraged, and the leader seeks to build consensus. Democratic leadership can lead to higher morale and stronger team cohesion, as individuals feel heard and respected.

- Transformational leaders focus on inspiring and motivating their teams to achieve extraordinary outcomes. They create a compelling vision of the future, align the team's efforts with that vision, and empower individuals to reach their full potential. Transformational leaders thrive on fostering innovation, driving change, and cultivating a sense of purpose within their teams. This style is particularly effective in environments requiring growth, adaptation, and long-term strategic thinking.

- Autocratic leaders take charge of decision-making and direct their teams with clear, authoritative instructions. This style can be beneficial in high-pressure situations where quick decisions are necessary, such as during crises or emergencies. While autocratic leadership can ensure efficiency and clarity, overuse of this approach may hinder creativity and lower team morale if team members feel their input is undervalued.

- Laissez-faire leadership emphasizes autonomy, granting team members the freedom to make decisions and solve problems independently. Leaders who adopt this style trust their team's expertise and prefer to take a "hands-off" approach. While this style works well with highly skilled and self-motivated teams, it may lead to confusion or inefficiency if team members lack direction or require additional support.

- Bureaucratic leaders rely on established processes, rules, and structures to guide their decision-making. This style is often seen in organizations where consistency, adherence to policies, and accountability are critical, such as government agencies or heavily regulated industries. While bureaucratic leadership provides clarity and reduces ambiguity, it may limit flexibility and slow down innovation in dynamic environments.

- Transactional leadership focuses on achieving specific tasks and objectives through structured roles, expectations, and rewards. Leaders in this style emphasize clear goals, well-defined processes, and performance-based recognition. Transactional leadership is effective in environments where short-term results and compliance with established standards are prioritized. However, it may lack the motivational and innovative elements necessary for long-term growth.

- Servant leaders prioritize the needs, growth, and well-being of their team members over their own authority. This approach emphasizes collaboration, empathy, and shared decision-making. Servant leadership builds trust, loyalty, and a positive team culture. Leaders who adopt this style focus on empowering individuals to excel, making it particularly effective in fostering strong interpersonal relationships and sustainable team development.

- Coaching leadership centers on mentorship, support, and encouragement. Leaders in this style take the time to understand the strengths, weaknesses, and aspirations of their team members, offering guidance to help them achieve their best outcomes. This approach creates a nurturing environment where individuals feel valued and are motivated to grow. Coaching leadership is especially effective in environments that prioritize personal and professional development.

CHOOSING THE RIGHT LEADERSHIP STYLE

The most effective leaders recognize that no single style is suitable for every situation. Instead, they adapt their approach based on their values, the dynamics of their team, and the specific goals they aim to achieve.

For example:

- Democratic leadership may be ideal for fostering creativity and innovation in collaborative settings.

- Transformational leadership is often necessary when driving significant organizational change or inspiring a sense of purpose.

- Autocratic leadership can be indispensable in emergencies requiring swift and decisive action.

- Servant leadership is valuable in building strong, people-centered teams with a focus on long-term growth.

Adapting leadership styles also involves self-awareness. A leader must evaluate their natural tendencies, strengths, and areas for improvement to determine which styles align best with their personality and values. Equally important is the ability to assess the needs of the team, objectives, and environment. Newly formed team may require more structure and direction, while an experienced, self-sufficient team might thrive under a laissez-faire or coaching approach.

Leaders who master the art of balancing and blending different styles create flexible, dynamic environments that encourage collaboration, innovation, and success. By remaining attuned to the changing needs of their teams and organizations, they ensure their leadership approach continues to resonate and deliver meaningful results.

SELF-LEADERSHIP

At the heart of effective leadership lies the principle of self-leadership—the ability to take ownership of your personal growth, mindset, and actions. Before you can guide others with integrity and purpose, you must first master the art of guiding yourself. Self-leadership is not merely a skill; it's a philosophy that informs every aspect of how you live, work, and interact with others. It can be demonstrated through: personal accountability, intentional growth, discipline, resilience, influence, and practice.

1. *Personal Accountability*

Great leaders recognize that their journey begins with a commitment to personal accountability. This means taking ownership and accepting responsibility for your actions, decisions, and outcomes—both successes and failures. It requires you to:

- Identify your values and use them as a compass for decision-making
- Acknowledge your strengths while addressing areas for growth
- Cultivate emotional intelligence to navigate challenges with self-awareness and empathy

By taking ownership, you demonstrate the courage to confront weaknesses, the humility to accept feedback, and the determination to pursue continuous self-improvement.

2. *Intentionality in Growth*

Self-leadership is grounded in intentionality—the deliberate effort to shape how you think, feel, and act in alignment with your goals and values. This involves:

- Clarifying your vision and purpose: Defining what matters most and what you aim to achieve
- Cultivating resilience: Building the mental and emotional strength to persevere through challenges and setbacks
- Aligning actions with goals: Ensuring that daily decisions contribute to long-term success

Intentionality requires you to be proactive, not reactive. Instead of being driven by external circumstances, self-leaders shape their environment and mindset to stay aligned with their goals. This approach fosters clarity, focus, and consistency.

3. Discipline

Effective self-leadership is built on the foundation of discipline. This means creating habits and routines that support personal and professional growth. Discipline involves:

- Setting realistic and measurable goals
- Prioritizing tasks and managing time effectively
- Holding yourself accountable for progress, even when motivation diminishes

Discipline is not about perfection; it's about persistence and operating in a standard of excellence by consistently aligning your actions with your intentions, you reinforce your commitment to self-leadership.

4. Resilience

Resilience is a cornerstone of self-leadership. It equips you to navigate the inevitable challenges, setbacks, and uncertainties of life. Cultivating resilience involves:

- Reframing failures as opportunities to learn and grow
- Practicing self-compassion to avoid burnout and maintain a positive outlook
- Building a support network to provide encouragement and perspective during tough times

Resilient leaders inspire others not by avoiding challenges, but by demonstrating the strength to rise above them.

5. Influence

Self-leadership is not only about personal growth; it is also about influence. When you lead yourself with purpose and integrity, you become a role model for others. By embodying the principles of accountability, intentionality, and discipline, you:

- Inspire confidence and trust in your leadership
- Create a culture of excellence and accountability
- Demonstrate that leadership is not a title, but a daily practice

Leaders who excel in self-leadership understand that their actions set the tone for their teams and organizations. By holding themselves to a high standard, they encourage others to do the same.

6. Practice

Self-leadership is not a one-time achievement; it's a lifelong journey of growth and refinement. It requires continuous reflection, learning, and adaptation. Leaders who embrace self-leadership commit to:

- Regularly assessing their performance
- Seeking feedback/ evaluations
- Adapting to new challenges and evolving their skills
- Remaining open to personal and professional development opportunities

Through self-leadership, you gain a deeper understanding of your identity, values, and vision as a leader. This clarity enables you to make intentional choices that inspire and empower others, creating a ripple effect of influence.

In mastering self-leadership, you lay the foundation for all other forms of leadership. It is a practice of aligning your internal values with your external actions, cultivating resilience and integrity, and becoming a guide for those around you. By leading yourself well, you can unlock your potential to lead others with authenticity and purpose.

THE WEIGHT OF LEADERSHIP: BARRIERS & LESSONS

Leadership often requires navigating complex barriers, making decisions that carry significant weight, and inspiring others to move toward a shared vision. The journey is rewarding, but not without its trials. The weight of leadership often tests a leader's resilience, integrity, and ability to adapt in the face of uncertainty. Understanding and embracing these challenges is what sets exceptional leaders apart.

Leadership often demands stepping out of one's comfort zone, confronting situations that test your confidence, and engaging with challenges that offer no easy solutions. These moments of discomfort can arise in various forms:

- *Addressing Conflict:* Whether resolving disputes between team members or navigating personal disagreements, addressing conflict requires emotional intelligence and the ability to mediate effectively.

- *Navigating Uncertainty:* Leaders frequently operate in unpredictable environments where clear answers are elusive. Making decisions with incomplete information is a hallmark of leadership.

- *Making Unpopular Decisions:* Sometimes, leaders must choose a path that isn't widely supported, but serves the greater good. These decisions can isolate leaders, but are necessary for long-term success.

Leaders often face discomfort. However, discomfort is not a sign of failure, but a catalyst for growth. It pushes leaders to develop new skills, expand their perspectives, and build resilience. Leaders who embrace discomfort see it as an opportunity to strengthen their character and refine their approach.

One of the most challenging aspects of leadership is making difficult decisions that impact individuals, teams, and organizations. These choices often require a delicate balance:

- *Empathy and Objectivity:* Understanding the personal impact of decisions while maintaining an objective perspective is key to earning trust and fostering fairness.

- *Short-term vs. Long-term Implications:* Tough decisions often involve trade-offs between immediate benefits and future outcomes. Effective leaders weigh these factors carefully, prioritizing sustainability and growth.

- *Facing Backlash:* Not all decisions will be met with unanimous approval. Leaders must have the courage to stand by their choices and address dissent constructively.

Every tough decision is an opportunity to demonstrate integrity and clarity. Leaders who approach these moments with empathy and transparency earn the respect of their teams, even in disagreement. Great leaders inspire their teams to believe in a vision and work toward it with enthusiasm. However, this is often easier said than done, especially when resistance arises:

- *Communicating a Clear Vision:* Effective leaders articulate a compelling vision that resonates with their teams, offering clarity and purpose.

- *Persistence in the Face of Resistance:* Not everyone will immediately align with a leader's goals or methods. Inspiring others requires patience, adaptability, and consistent encouragement.

- *Leading by Example:* Actions speak louder than words. Leaders who embody the values they promote inspire confidence and commitment from their teams.

The challenges of leadership may be intense, but so are the lessons they offer. Each trial serves as an opportunity to deepen self-awareness, strengthen resolve, and refine skills. Leaders who embrace these challenges with humility and determination not only grow themselves, but also inspire those around them to do the same.

The weight of leadership is not a burden to be avoided, but a responsibility to be embraced. It is through these challenges—discomfort, tough decisions, and inspiring others—that leaders discover their true potential and leave a lasting legacy. By approaching leadership with empathy, clarity, and resilience, leaders create environments where individuals and teams can thrive, united by a shared purpose and vision.

LEGACY LEADERSHIP: CREATING A LASTING IMPACT

Leadership that leaves a legacy is leadership that transcends the immediate and creates a wave of positive change. Legacy leadership is about influencing people, organizations, and communities in ways that endure long after you've moved on. It is the ability to instill values, inspire growth, and establish systems that empower others to continue achieving and innovating. Legacy leaders focus not only on their own achievements, but on laying the groundwork for those who follow, ensuring sustained progress and impact.

Legacy leadership requires intentionality. It is a commitment to aligning your daily actions, decisions, and interactions with a vision that reflects your core values and purpose. This form of leadership asks leaders to consider their broader influence—how their efforts contribute to the growth of individuals, the strength of their organizations, and the betterment of society.

At its core, legacy leadership is not about the leader's success, but about the success they enable for others. It's about fostering a culture of empowerment, vision, and continuous improvement that inspires individuals to rise to their fullest potential.

To build a meaningful legacy as a leader, you must integrate specific principles into your approach:

Align Actions with Values

Legacy leaders consistently act in ways that reflect their long-term vision and deeply held beliefs. Every choice, no matter how small, contributes to the larger narrative of who they are and what they stand for. This alignment creates trust and sets an example for others to follow. When actions align with values, leaders inspire confidence, credibility, and purpose.

Foster Empowerment

Great leaders help cultivate success in others. Legacy leaders create an environment where team members feel valued, capable, and motivated to excel. They provide the tools, resources, and encouragement needed for individuals to take ownership of their growth. Empowerment is about instilling confidence and agency, enabling others to thrive and continue the mission even in the leader's absence.

Invest in Relationships

Authentic connections are the cornerstone of legacy leadership. Building relationships based on trust, mutual respect, and genuine care creates a supportive environment where people feel seen, heard, and valued. Legacy leaders take the time to understand those they lead, creating community and belonging. These connections often outlast formal roles, creating networks of influence and collaboration.

Lead with Vision

Legacy leaders inspire others by painting a clear picture of a meaningful future. They articulate a purpose that resonates, mobilizing teams to work together toward shared goals. A compelling vision not only unites individuals, but also ensures that efforts are directed toward outcomes that matter. Visionary leaders leave behind a sense of purpose that continues to guide others after their tenure.

Embrace Change

The ability to adapt is crucial for legacy leaders. They recognize that progress often requires innovation, disruption, and flexibility. Embracing change involves being open to new ideas, fostering a culture of experimentation, and leading with resilience through uncertainty. By modeling adaptability, legacy leaders prepare their organizations and communities to thrive in an ever-changing world.

Share Knowledge

Legacy leadership is rooted in the idea of giving back. By mentoring others and sharing insights, legacy leaders equip future generations with the tools, wisdom, and inspiration needed to succeed. They prioritize teaching over telling, focusing on cultivating independent thinkers and confident problem-solvers. Shared knowledge becomes the foundation upon which others can build, ensuring that progress continues.

Legacy leadership should never be about personal accolades or fleeting achievements— it should focus on creating systems, cultures, and relationships that endure. A legacy leader's influence can be seen in:

- The empowerment of individuals who go on to achieve their own successes
- The establishment of sustainable processes and systems that continue to deliver results
- The fostering of values-driven cultures that align with purpose and integrity
- The ripple effect of shared wisdom, where lessons learned are passed down and multiplied

Legacy leadership is not something you create at the end of your journey; it is something you build every day. Every decision, interaction, and initiative contributes to the legacy you leave behind. By focusing on the principles of alignment, empowerment, relationship-building, vision, adaptability, and knowledge-sharing, you ensure that your influence will continue to inspire and uplift others.

To leave a meaningful legacy as a leader, commit to growth not only for yourself, but for those around you. Invest in people, create systems that outlast your tenure, and lead with purpose and integrity. In doing so, you create a lasting impact that transforms lives, organizations, and communities, leaving the world better than you found it.

PERSONAL LESSONS: MY LEADERSHIP JOURNEY

Leadership is an ongoing journey of growth, learning, and self-discovery. As I reflect on my experiences, I see how the various roles I've played—both personal and professional—have shaped my understanding of what it truly means to lead. Each step in this journey, whether marked by triumph or challenge, has deepened my appreciation for the complexities and rewards of leadership.

From an early age, leadership was woven into my life, even before I fully recognized it. As the eldest sibling, I naturally stepped into a leadership role within my family. Guiding my siblings through life's challenges required resilience, empathy, and the ability to adapt quickly. These moments taught me that leadership isn't about authority or titles; it's about stepping up when others look to you for guidance.

Later, as I transitioned into professional roles, leadership became more formalized. I was tasked with creating visions, rallying teams, and making decisions that would impact not only my career, but also the lives and growth of those I led. In these moments, I came to understand that leadership is about service—about empowering others to reach their potential while navigating the complexities of shared goals.

Leadership often required me to step into uncomfortable spaces. There were times when I had to make decisions that were unpopular, navigate conflicts within teams, or confront my own uncertainties about whether I was equipped to lead. These moments were not easy, but they were necessary. They pushed me out of my comfort zone and challenged me to grow in ways I hadn't anticipated.

One of the most difficult aspects of leadership can be making tough decisions, naviagating systemic barriers especially when those decisions impact people you care about. Balancing the needs of individuals with the greater good of the organization or community is a delicqate task, often requiring clarity, empathy, and courage. In these moments, I learned the importance of authenticity—of staying true to my values and being transparent about the reasoning behind my choices.

Doubt was another challenge I faced. There were times when I questioned whether I had the answers or the strength to lead effectively. But I came to realize that leadership isn't about having all the answers; it's about being willing to ask the right questions, seek out the best solutions, and guide others toward a collective vision. It's about being human, acknowledging your limitations, and demonstrating the courage to grow alongside your team.

Through these challenges, I learned that humility is one of the most powerful tools a leader can possess. Leadership isn't about being the smartest person in the room or asserting dominance—it's about listening, learning, and valuing the contributions of others. Humility allows you to admit when you're wrong, seek input from those around you, and build trust through vulnerability.

Perseverance also became a cornerstone of my leadership philosophy. There were times when the path forward was unclear, when setbacks threatened to derail progress, or when resistance seemed insurmountable. In these moments, I leaned on my vision and the shared purpose of the team to keep moving forward. I discovered that resilience isn't just about pushing through challenges—it's about adapting, staying focused, and maintaining hope, even in the face of uncertainty.

Despite its challenges, leadership is incredibly rewarding. There is no greater joy than witnessing the growth and success of those you've had the privilege to lead. Whether it's a team member achieving a goal they once thought impossible, a group coming together to overcome a significant obstacle, or an individual stepping into their own leadership potential, these moments reaffirm the purpose of leadership.

Leadership is fundamentally about people. It's about building relationships, creating spaces where others feel valued and supported, and fostering an environment where growth is possible. The trust and collaboration that emerge from these connections are powerful, creating a ripple effect of positive change.

For me, the most fulfilling aspect of leadership is seeing others succeed—not because of my efforts alone, but because of the collective energy and dedication of the team. Leadership is not about taking credit; it's about sharing it, amplifying the voices of others, and celebrating their achievements.

As I continue my journey, I've come to embrace leadership as a dynamic and evolving practice. It requires self-awareness, intentionality, and a commitment to continuous growth. Each experience, whether a success or a setback, adds to my leadership story. These moments have taught me that leadership isn't just about guiding others—it's about learning from them as well.

Through this journey, I've discovered that leadership is less about perfection and more about progress. It's about being willing to step into uncertainty, navigate discomfort, and remain steadfast in your values and vision. It's about lifting others up, creating opportunities for them to shine, and building a legacy that endures long after your role has ended.

Leadership, at its heart, is a journey of service, growth, and impact. It's a journey I am honored to walk and one that continues to teach me the power of humility, resilience, and shared purpose. As I reflect on my experiences, I am reminded that leadership is not just about the destination—it's about the lives you touch and the lessons you carry along the way.

LEADERSHIP REVIEW

Leadership is a continuous process of learning, growing, and evolving. It is a calling that demands courage to step into uncertainty, empathy to understand and connect with others, and the resilience to adapt in the face of challenges, knowing that the change will follow. True leadership is not confined to moments of authority; it is found in everyday acts of inspiration, guidance, and service.

1. **Leadership is dynamic.** It grows and transforms as we do, shaped by our experiences, values, and the relationships we cultivate along the way. It requires humility to acknowledge that we do not have all the answers and the openness to learn from those we lead. The journey of leadership challenges us to continuously refine our vision, sharpen our skills, and expand our capacity to influence and inspire.

2. **At its core, leadership begins with self-leadership.** The ability to take ownership of your story, your values, and your purpose. Before we can guide others, we must lead ourselves with discipline, self-awareness, and intention. Self-leadership is about aligning your actions with your core beliefs, setting an example through your choices, and committing to personal growth. It is a practice of authenticity, showing up as your true self and encouraging others to do the same.

3. **True leadership extends far beyond self.** It is about empowering others to realize their potential, fostering an environment where individuals feel valued, supported, and capable of achieving their best. Leadership is not about controlling outcomes, but about inspiring a shared vision, providing guidance, and creating opportunities for growth. It is about building bridges, nurturing trust, and lifting others as you climb.

4. **Leadership thrives on relationships.** The connections we make with others form the foundation of our ability to lead effectively. By listening deeply, communicating openly, and valuing diverse perspectives, we create a sense of unity and

shared purpose. These meaningful connections enable leaders to inspire collective action, navigate challenges with empathy, and build lasting bonds that extend beyond immediate goals.

5. At its highest expression, leadership is about legacy. It is the imprint we leave on people, organizations, and communities long after we have moved on. Legacy leadership is not just about accomplishments; it is about the values we instill, the opportunities we create, and the lives we touch. It is about ensuring that the impact of our leadership endures, empowering others to continue the work we began.

6. In every role—whether formal or informal—leadership is an opportunity to make a difference. It calls on us to take ownership of our responsibilities, embrace challenges with grace, and lead with integrity, vision, and heart. Leadership is not about perfection; it is about progress. It is about daring to dream, to take risks, and to inspire others to do the same.

As leaders, we are entrusted with the privilege of guiding and uplifting others. This is both a responsibility and an honor, one that requires us to lead with authenticity, compassion, and purpose.

Let us embrace the essence of leadership, committing ourselves to the ongoing work of self-discovery, empowerment, and service. Let us lead with courage and integrity, always striving to make a positive difference in the lives of those we touch. And let us remember that true leadership is not about the power we hold, but the legacy we live and leave behind.

LEADERSHIP IN ACTION

Leadership is about taking initiative, inspiring others, and making a difference wherever you are. This application section provides practical ways to integrate the principles of leadership into your daily life, empowering you to lead with purpose and authenticity.

1. Take Ownership of Your Role

- Identify one area in your life—personal, professional, or community-focused—where you can take responsibility. This might mean improving communication at work, fostering positivity in your family, or mentoring someone in need.

- **Action Step:** Write down one specific goal you want to achieve in this area and the first step you'll take to make progress.

2. Practice Self-Leadership

- Leadership starts within. Develop self-awareness by reflecting on your values, strengths, and areas for growth. Set boundaries and create habits that align with your goals.

- **Action Step:** Spend time in the evening journaling about your day, noting what went well and what could be improved.

3. Empower Others

- Great leaders inspire others to achieve their potential.

Look for opportunities to mentor, encourage, or provide resources to those around you.

- **Action Step:** Reach out to a colleague, friend, or family member this week and offer your support or guidance in an area they're navigating.

4. Be Adaptable and Resilient

- Leadership requires flexibility in the face of challenges. When setbacks occur, focus on solutions rather than problems.

- **Action Step:** The next time you face a challenge, write down three possible solutions before reacting.

5. Communicate Effectively

- Leadership relies on clear, empathetic communication. Practice active listening, ask thoughtful questions, and ensure your message aligns with your values.

- **Action Step:** During your next important conversation, listen without interrupting and summarize what you heard before responding.

LEADERSHIP CHALLENGE

Reflect on self-leadership in your life on a weekly basis to ensure you have what you need to thrive. Also, identify your current leadership style and how it shows up in your daily life. Reflect on your experience and journal about the following:

- What did I do to lead in this situation?
- How did my actions impact myself and others?
- What did I learn about leadership from this experience?

_____
_____
_____
_____
_____
_____
_____
_____
_____
_____
_____
_____
_____
_____
_____
_____
_____
_____
_____
_____
_____
_____

2

EDUCATION

E ducation goes beyond being an accumulation of facts; it is the path to empowerment and freedom. It offers the tools to navigate life's challenges, disrupt societal limitations, and reshape our narratives. Education instills confidence, widens perspectives, and fosters a sense of purpose.

For me, the journey of education was transformative. It was a gateway that not only unlocked new opportunities, but also altered the way I viewed the world and my place within it. Education empowered me to confront barriers—both external and internal—and to rewrite the story of what was possible for someone like me.

KNOWLEDGE AS EMPOWERMENT

The phrase "people perish from a lack of knowledge" is a profound truth that underscores the role of education in shaping lives, communities, and futures. Ignorance confines individuals to the limits of what they already know, while knowledge serves as a gateway to possibility, progress, and purpose. Education—whether acquired formally through institutions or informally through lived experiences—is a transformative force that equips individuals to dream, innovate, and achieve.

For many, education is not a given; it is a hard-won privilege. The barriers to education are often significant and multifaceted: financial hardships, systemic inequities, societal expectations, and even internalized doubt. These obstacles create a reality where access to education is unequal, making the pursuit of knowledge a deliberate and often challenging endeavor. Yet, those who overcome these barriers discover a transformative power that extends far beyond the classroom. Education becomes a foundation upon which new futures are built and oppressive systems are dismantled.

The empowerment that comes with knowledge is both personal and collective. On a personal level, education fosters self-awareness, resilience, and confidence. Each lesson learned, each skill acquired becomes a tool for navigating life's challenges and carving out opportunities. Education enables individuals to break free from limiting narratives, proving that their potential is not confined by their circumstances, but expanded by their willingness to learn and grow.

Collectively, education empowers communities by fostering critical thinking and inspiring action. It challenges societal norms, disrupts cycles of oppression, and provides individuals with the tools to advocate for change. Education cultivates leaders, innovators, and problem-solvers who can reimagine the systems that perpetuate inequity. For those of us who have experienced systemic barriers firsthand, education becomes not just a personal journey, but a means of contributing to broader social progress.

For me, education was a transformative lens through which I began to understand the world and my place within it. It gave me the language to articulate the challenges I faced and the tools to envision solutions. Through education, I was able to critically examine the systemic issues that had shaped my life—issues like the education-to-prison pipeline, redlining, and generational poverty. Understanding these systems not only gave me clarity, but also empowered me to take action, whether by advocating for others, creating initiatives, or pursuing paths that once seemed out of reach.

Education's power lies in its ability to expand perspectives and push boundaries. It forces us to question what we think we know and invites us to explore new possibilities. It encourages curiosity, fosters innovation, and instills a sense of agency. Through education, I was able to see the world not as a fixed reality, but as a canvas for change—one where I could contribute, create, and make a difference.

The fight for education is worth every challenge, not because it guarantees success, but because it empowers individuals to define success on their own terms. It provides the skills, confidence, and vision needed to overcome barriers and build a future that reflects one's values and aspirations. For those of us who have had to fight for our right to learn, education becomes a testament to our resilience and a reminder of the limitless potential that lies within us.

Ultimately, education is an act of liberation. It liberates us from ignorance, from the limitations imposed by others, and from the fear of what lies beyond our current understanding. It empowers us to imagine, to innovate, and to inspire. And in doing so, it transforms not only individuals, but entire communities, leaving a legacy of possibility for generations to come.

BREAKING BARRIERS THROUGH EDUCATION

The path to education was a battle against deeply entrenched barriers, both external and internal. As a first-generation student, I faced an uphill climb that required resilience, determination, and a refusal to accept the limitations imposed on me. Education, for me, became a personal revolution—a way to rewrite the narrative that society had written for me and others like me.

Growing up in a marginalized community meant being inundated with stereotypes and assumptions about what I could achieve. These stereotypes were not just casual remarks, but systemic messages embedded in educational institutions, societal expectations, and even well-meaning advice. They told me that my dreams were too big, that I wasn't smart enough, prepared enough, or worthy enough to claim success as my own. These narratives were designed to make me shrink, to accept less than what I knew I was capable of achieving.

Yet, I chose not to internalize these messages. Instead, I saw education as my way to challenge them head-on. Every decision to keep moving forward—whether it was filling out scholarship applications, navigating complex financial aid systems, or balancing school with work and family responsibilities—was a step towards liberation. Each step forward was proof that I could not only survive in spaces that weren't designed for me, but thrive in them.

The systemic inequities I encountered were unrelenting. As a Black woman in predominantly white academic spaces, I faced microaggressions and biases that often left me feeling invisible or hyper-visible, depending on the moment. I was frequently expected to speak on behalf of my entire race, as if my experiences were a pillar. These experiences ranged from dismissive comments about my capabilities to outright skepticism about my presence in those spaces. Such moments were isolating, making me question whether I truly belonged. Yet, each time I felt silenced, I found ways to amplify my voice—whether through persistence, advocacy, or academic excellence.

Financial challenges were another constant hurdle. The cost of higher education often felt overwhelming, especially for someone from a low-income background. Scholarships, while helpful, came with their own complexities—stringent requirements, limited availability, and decisions that didn't always align with my needs or goals. Student loans loomed as a necessary burden, a reminder of the price I was paying to pursue a better future. These financial pressures were discouraging, but I refused to let them dictate my path. Instead, I sought out every possible resource, juggled jobs, and learned to manage my finances strategically to ensure I could continue my education.

Breaking barriers also required me to challenge the expectations placed on me by society—and by myself. Growing up, I had internalized the idea that failure was final, that setbacks defined my worth. But as I progressed through my educational journey, I began to unlearn this damaging mindset. I realized that failure was not a mark of inadequacy, but part of a journey that led to growth. Each setback was an opportunity to recalibrate, to learn, and to come back stronger. This shift in perspective allowed me to persevere through challenges that might have otherwise derailed me.

The emotional toll of breaking barriers was significant. There were moments of doubt, exhaustion, and frustration. Yet, within those moments, I found strength. I leaned on mentors, peers, and my own solid belief that education was worth the struggle. I reminded myself that each step forward wasn't just for me—it was for everyone who had ever been told they weren't enough and for those who would come after me, walking paths made easier by the barriers I had helped to dismantle.

Through education, I discovered the power of self-advocacy. I learned to ask for what I needed, to navigate systems that weren't designed with me in mind, and to assert my value in spaces that often questioned it. These lessons extended far beyond the classroom, shaping the way I approached challenges in every aspect of my life.

Ultimately, breaking barriers through education was about redefining what was possible. It was about proving to myself and others that the limitations placed on me were not truths, but challenges to be overcome. And in doing so, I found not just knowledge, but empowerment, liberation, and the courage to inspire others to do the same.

LIFELONG LEARNING: A JOURNEY WITHOUT END

Education is not confined to the walls of a classroom or the pages of a textbook. It is a continuous, evolving process—a journey of discovery that extends throughout our lives. Lifelong learning embraces the idea that growth is fueled by curiosity, experience, and an unyielding desire to evolve. For me, this concept has been transformative, shaping not only my academic pursuits, but also my approach to life itself.

Lifelong learning goes beyond the pursuit of degrees or formal qualifications; it is about cultivating a mindset of curiosity and adaptability. It means recognizing that every moment, every experience, and every interaction offers an opportunity to learn, grow, and refine our understanding of the world. Consider the following tools of education:

1. Books

Books have been my most steadfast companions on this journey, offering windows into worlds beyond my own and language to articulate my experiences. They have been a source of wisdom, empowerment, and perspective, helping me to see my life within the context of broader social, historical, and cultural narratives. Books have equipped me with tools to challenge injustices, advocate for change, and envision new possibilities.

Through the pages of books, I have explored the resilience of others who overcame barriers similar to mine, learning from their victories and struggles. They have provided not just knowledge, but also the courage to persist, reminding me that I am not alone in my journey. Each book has been a building block, expanding my worldview and reinforcing my belief in the power of education to transform lives.

2. Mentorship

Mentors have played a pivotal role in my lifelong learning journey. These individuals have been guides, cheerleaders, and sometimes mirrors reflecting the potential I couldn't always see in myself. They've offered practical advice, shared valuable insights, and provided emotional support when the road felt especially challenging. Their belief in me has been a driving force, encouraging me to take risks, embrace growth, and step into opportunities that once felt out of reach.

Mentorship has taught me the importance of community and reciprocity in education. Just as I have been uplifted by the knowledge and guidance of others, I strive to pass that torch by mentoring those who come after me. Sharing knowledge goes beyond an act of generosity; it is a way to multiply impact and ensure that learning becomes a collective journey.

3. Experience

While books and mentors have provided invaluable knowl-edge and guidance, experience has been my greatest teacher. Hands-on opportunities, whether through internships, community engagement, or leadership roles, have been where theory meets practice. These experiences have allowed me to test what I've learned, adapt to real-world challenges, and discover my strengths in action.

Through community involvement, I've seen firsthand the power of collective effort and the importance of under-standing diverse perspectives. Internships have given me practical skills and insights that no classroom could fully replicate, clarifying my goals and showing me how to navigate the complexities of professional and social systems. Every experience, whether a triumph or a setback, has deepened my understanding of myself and my purpose.

4. Curiosity

At the heart of lifelong learning is a spirit of curiosity—a hunger to understand, to question, and to grow. This curiosity has led me to explore new fields, challenge my assumptions, and seek out diverse perspectives. It has taught me that learning thrives on openness and a willingness to embrace change.

Lifelong learning is about using the knowledge gained to make an impact. For me, the lessons I've learned have been tools not only for navigating my own journey, but also for uplifting those around me. They've shown me that the pursuit of knowledge is as much about contributing to the world as it is about understanding it.

Lifelong learning has shown me that education is not something we complete—it is something we live. Each chapter of life offers new lessons, challenges, and opportunities to grow. Whether through reading, mentorship, or direct experience, learning never truly ends. It evolves with us, adapting to our changing needs and aspirations.

This journey has been both humbling and empowering, reminding me that no matter how much I've learned, there is always more to discover. It's a reminder that education is not just about gaining knowledge, but about becoming more thoughtful, compassionate, and engaged with the world around us. Lifelong learning has taught me that growth is limitless—and that is a lesson I will carry with me forever.

THE TRANSFORMATIVE POWER OF EDUCATION

Education is a force that reshapes lives, ignites potential, and empowers individuals to reimagine what is possible. It holds the power to liberate—not just from ignorance, but from the limitations imposed by systemic oppression and societal expectations. For those of us from marginalized communities, education becomes both a weapon and a shield, equipping us to dismantle barriers, rewrite narratives, and carve out spaces where our voices can no longer be ignored.

The process of learning transformed not only my circumstances, but my mindset. It taught me to question the status quo, to recognize the systems and structures that perpetuate inequality, and to see myself as a change-maker within those systems. With each degree earned and skill mastered, I felt a growing sense of empowerment. I was no longer just surviving; I was actively shaping my future.

One of the most profound gifts education gave me was the ability to understand and articulate the mechanisms of power and exclusion. I learned the language of systems designed to exclude people like me—systems that often operate under the guise of neutrality, but are steeped in bias. By understanding these systems, I could challenge their inequities, both for myself and for those who would come after me.

This knowledge was deeply personal. Education gave me the ability to name my experiences, to recognize the microaggressions, the biases, and the systemic barriers that had shaped my journey. Armed with this understanding, I became better equipped to advocate for change—not only for myself, but for my community. Education transformed me into a voice for equity and justice in spaces that often resisted such voices.

The true power of education lies not just in what it allows us to achieve individually, but in its capacity to uplift others. My journey through education was fueled by the belief that my success could pave the way for others. Each milestone was not just a personal victory, but a collective one—a step toward breaking generational cycles of oppression and creating new possibilities for those who shared my struggles.

Education gave me the confidence to mentor, guide, and inspire others to pursue their own paths of liberation. It showed me that knowledge is not meant to be hoarded, but shared. By opening doors for others, I was able to extend the impact of my education beyond my own life.

The path to educational success was not without its hardships. As a first-generation student navigating predominantly white institutions, I faced moments of isolation, microaggressions, and self-doubt. There were times when the sacrifices—financial, emotional, and mental—felt overwhelming. The weight of systemic oppression was a constant companion, reminding me that the spaces I entered were not designed with me in mind.

Yet, even in those moments of doubt, I held onto the belief that education was worth the struggle. I reminded myself that every challenge I overcame was a victory against a system that sought to limit me. Education became my act of defiance, my way of proving that I was not defined by the barriers placed in my path.

For me, education continues to be a pathway of freedom and hope. It shows me that I have the power to shape my own destiny, no matter how formidable the odds.

Education transformed not only my opportunities, but also my sense of self. It taught me that I am capable, resilient, and deserving of a seat at the table. It gave me the courage to demand more—not just for myself, but for those who look to me as an example of what is possible.

As I reflect on my journey, I see education as a bridge—a connection between where I started and where I aspire to go. It has been a catalyst for growth, a source of empowerment, and a reminder that even in the face of adversity, transformation is always within reach.

EMPOWERING OTHERS THROUGH EDUCATION

One of the most fulfilling aspects of my educational journey has been the opportunity to empower others. Education has never been just about my own achievements; it has always been about creating a ripple effect—sharing the lessons, resources, and opportunities I've gained to uplift others. This commitment to empowering others stems from a deep understanding of the transformative power of education and the belief that when one of us rises, we all rise.

Education is a collective tool for breaking cycles of poverty, dismantling systemic barriers, and building stronger, more equitable communities. Each degree earned, each barrier overcome, and each skill acquired can inspire someone else to believe in their own potential. The knowledge and opportunities I've gained aren't meant to be hoarded, but shared, creating a ripple effect that touches lives beyond my own.

I've seen firsthand how education can shift the trajectory of not just individuals, but entire families and communities. By mentoring, advocating, and sharing resources, I've worked to ensure that others can access the same transformative opportunities I fought to achieve. Each act of empowerment—whether helping someone navigate the complexities of financial aid or encouraging them to dream bigger than their circumstances—creates a chain reaction that has the potential to reshape futures.

The cornerstone of my commitment to empowering others is mentorship. As someone who has navigated the challenges of being a first-generation college student and a Black woman in predominantly white institutions, I've made it my mission to guide others through similar journeys. I understand the isolation, doubt, and systemic barriers they face, and I strive to be a source of encouragement, guidance, inspiration, and reassurance.

Mentorship is about listening, validating experiences, and helping others see the strength within themselves. Whether it's offering advice on career paths, connecting students with scholarships, or simply being a sounding board, I see mentorship as a way to ensure that others don't have to face the same struggles alone.

Advocacy has been equally important in my efforts to empower others. I've worked to challenge the inequities within educational systems, pushing for policies that promote diversity, inclusion, and accessibility. From addressing financial barriers to advocating for culturally responsive teaching practices, my goal has been to create environments where all students can thrive, regardless of their background or circumstances.

Education is a community endeavor. By investing in others, we strengthen the fabric of our communities and create a cycle of empowerment that benefits future generations. I've worked to build programs and initiatives that provide resources, guidance, and support for students from underrepresented backgrounds. These efforts are about creating a culture of possibility where success is attainable for all.

Whether it's implementing workshops, bridging the access gap, creating innovative experiences, connecting students with mentors, or simply sharing my own story, I see every interaction as an opportunity to inspire. Each person I empower has the potential to empower others, creating a tangible effect far beyond what I can see. This cycle of empowerment is what drives me to keep pushing for change, even in the face of resistance.

Empowering others through education is a reminder that our journeys are interconnected. Every barrier I've broken, every lesson I've learned, and every opportunity I've seized has been made possible by the sacrifices and support of those who came before me. In turn, I see it as my responsibility to pave the way for those who come after me.

This work isn't always easy. Empowering others often means confronting systemic barriers, challenging deeply ingrained biases, and working tirelessly to create spaces where everyone can thrive. But it's also deeply rewarding. Seeing someone I've mentored achieve their goals, watching a student overcome challenges to reach their potential, or knowing that my advocacy has contributed to a more equitable system is a source of profound fulfillment.

Education is a tool for liberation, but it's also a tool for connection. By sharing knowledge, resources, and encouragement, we create a cycle of empowerment that extends beyond ourselves. This cycle doesn't just benefit individuals; it transforms communities, creates opportunities, and fosters a more just and equitable society.

Empowering others through education is a lifelong commitment. It's a call to invest in people, to believe in their potential, and to work collectively to break down barriers. By doing so, we not only change lives—we create a legacy of empowerment that will continue to inspire and uplift for generations to come.

PERSONAL APPLICATION

Education is the ultimate form of liberation. It is the bridge between what is and what can be, offering us the tools to challenge the status quo, envision a better future, and actively create the change we wish to see in the world. Education has served as a means of personal achievement—a transformative journey of self-discovery, resilience, and purpose.

Through education, I have found the strength to navigate and dismantle the systemic barriers that sought to limit me. It has taught me the power of perseverance, the importance of critical thinking, and the value of self-belief. More than that, education has shown me that knowledge is not just for individual gain—it is a powerful force for collective empowerment and social transformation.

Education has been a lens through which I have come to understand not only the world, but also myself. It has revealed my strengths, exposed my vulnerabilities, and shaped my vision for the future. The journey has been anything, but easy, filled with obstacles that tested my resolve. Yet, it is in overcoming those challenges that I discovered resilience, the ability to adapt and thrive even in the face of adversity.

The lessons I've learned through education extend far beyond the classroom. They are lessons of identity, community, and purpose. Education has allowed me to explore who I am, where I come from, and what I am capable of achieving. It has given me the confidence to rewrite my narrative, to redefine what is possible, and to push the boundaries of what I once believed I could achieve.

The pursuit of education does not end with a diploma or degree. True education is a continuous process of growth, fueled by curiosity, reflection, and the desire to evolve. It calls us to remain students of life, open to new perspectives, willing to challenge old beliefs, and ready to embrace the unknown.

As I continue on this journey, I am committed to the idea that learning is never complete. Education is a collective responsibility. It equips us to contribute to our communities, challenge injustices, advocate for ourselves and those who have been silenced or marginalized. The true power of education lies in its ability to uplift not just individuals, but entire generations. It enables us to dismantle systemic oppression, bridge divides, and create spaces where everyone has the opportunity to thrive.

Education holds the promise of freedom—not just from ignorance, but from the constraints that prevent us from reaching our full potential. It empowers us to question, to imagine, and to act. It gives us the language to articulate our dreams, the tools to realize them, and the courage to pursue them, even in the face of doubt.

With every lesson learned, every challenge overcome, and every barrier broken, we come closer to fulfilling the true promise of education. It is a promise not only of personal transformation, but of societal progress. It is a call to action—to use what we have learned to uplift, to inspire, and to create a world where the transformative power of education is accessible to all.

Education is the light that guides us through the darkness of limitation, ignorance, and inequity. It is the key that unlocks doors to opportunity, the foundation for innovation, and the spark that ignites change. And as we continue to learn, grow, and empower others, we honor education's highest purpose: to create a more just, equitable, and liberated world.

EDUCATION IN ACTION

To integrate the principles of education into your daily life, focus on intentional learning. This means not only pursuing formal education when needed, but also finding informal opportunities to grow. Whether it's through books, podcasts, online courses, or conversations with mentors, learning should align with your purpose and expand your perspective.

Here are actionable ways to incorporate education into your daily routine:

1. **Set Clear Learning Goals:** Identify an area of your life where you feel you need growth or new skills. Write down what you hope to achieve and why it's important.

2. **Find Resources:** Seek out books, courses, mentors, or communities that align with your goals. Choose resources that challenge you and encourage deeper understanding.

3. **Create a Learning Habit:** Dedicate a specific time each day or week for intentional learning. It could be 30 minutes of reading, an online tutorial, or engaging in meaningful discussions.

4. **Apply What You Learn:** Knowledge becomes valuable when it's put into action. Find ways to use new skills or insights in your personal or professional life.

5. **Reflect on Progress:** Take time to evaluate how your learning journey is impacting your mindset, skills, and growth. Adjust your goals and methods, as needed.

EDUCATION CHALLENGE

Identify a goal you have – informal or formal– and do some action research to create stepping stones. Use the following challenges to put the principles of education into practice that align with the learning enrichment goal you are focusing on.

1. **Enroll in a Course or Workshop:** Sign up for a learning opportunity that aligns with your goals—this could be professional, personal, or skill-based.

2. **Start a Knowledge Journal:** Dedicate a notebook to track insights from books, articles, or discussions that inspire you.

3. **Join a Learning Community:** Find a group, club, or online community where you can exchange ideas and learn collaboratively.

Reflect on your experience and journal about the following:

- What new insights or skills have you learned?
- What patterns or recurring themes have you noticed?
- What value have you gained from this experience?
- What stepping stones are needed to accomplish the goal?

_____
_____
_____
_____
_____
_____
_____
_____
_____
_____

3
GROWTH

Growth is often born from discomfort, failure, and pain. It's in these moments that we are forced to confront our vulnerabilities, challenge our limitations, and rise above circumstances that threaten to hold us back. Growth is not merely an outcome, but a choice—an ongoing process of resilience, transformation, and finding purpose in adversity.

Throughout my life, I have come to understand that growth requires us to lean into the discomfort of change and embrace the challenges that stretch us beyond our comfort zones. It is through these moments of difficulty that we discover our strength, refine our purpose, and create opportunities to flourish. Growth is a testament to the human spirit's ability to persevere and evolve, even in the face of overwhelming odds.

PERSONAL GROWTH: RESILIENCE IN ADVERSITY

Personal growth is a journey of transformation, requiring us to develop mentally, emotionally, spiritually, and physically. It demands an honest look at who we are and a commitment to becoming the best versions of ourselves. For me, personal growth became an act of defiance against the challenges and circumstances, that sought to define me. I chose to see each obstacle not as a barrier, but as an opportunity for holistic transformation which allowed me to address the root of the issues that arose.

True growth begins with self-reflection to become more self-aware. This an unflinching willingness to understand our values, beliefs, behaviors, and the narratives we carry. Self-awareness is not about judgment— it is about clarity. By reflecting on my actions and thoughts, I was able to identify the emotional and mental weights I carried, such as abandonment, rejection, misunderstanding, unpro-tection, and a tendency to internalize my input or feelings for others.

Acknowledging my blind spots was humbling, but necessary. It forced me to confront the ways I held myself back and allowed me to embrace the potential within me. Through self-awareness, I began to set intentional goals, align my actions with my values, be a woman of my word, operate in integrity, and recognize the parts of myself that needed nurturing. This clarity became the foundation for every step I took on my journey of growth.

Personal growth also requires resilience. Resilience is often seen as the ability to bounce back from adversity, but it is also about learning to navigate the emotional landscapes of our lives. It doesn't mean ignoring pain or pretending everything is fine. Instead, resilience means acknowledging our emotions, understanding their root causes, and using them as fuel for transformation.

For me, this meant confronting feelings of inadequacy, fear of failure, and the rejection that had shaped much of my inner dialogue. I learned that resilience required grace—not just for others, but for myself. I allowed myself to grieve losses, celebrate progress, and move forward even when the path was unclear.

One of the most significant lessons I learned was that growth has many twists and turns. There were days when progress felt tangible, and others when it felt elusive. By embracing this reality, I was able to cultivate patience and persistence, understanding that every step —no matter how small—was part of a larger process.

Furthermore, personal growth does not happen in isolation. The way we relate to others plays a significant role in our development. I learned that fostering healthy relationships required me to first establish a healthy relationship with myself. This meant setting boundaries that protected my well-being, communicating openly about my needs, and learning to trust both myself and others.

In my journey, I came to understand that growth is a shared experience. By supporting others in their journeys, I found that my own growth deepened. Whether it was through acts of mentorship, collaboration, or simply being present, I discovered the transformative power of having a community of care. Supporting others helped me recognize the importance of empathy, mutual respect, and the ability to celebrate collective progress.

At the same time, I had to learn the importance of honoring my own growth even when others did not acknowledge it. This meant recognizing when relationships were no longer healthy or aligned with my values and having the courage to let them go. Growth often requires difficult decisions, but it also brings clarity about the kind of relationships that nurture and inspire us.

The journey of personal growth is not about reaching a destination; it is about continuously evolving. It requires self-awareness to assess where we are, resilience to navigate the challenges we face, and a commitment to nurturing both ourselves and others. For me, personal growth became a way to reclaim control over my life, proving that our circumstances do not define us—our choices do. With each step forward, I discovered not only who I was, but also the limitless potential of who I could become.

EMBRACING DISCOMFORT FOR PROGRESS

Professional growth is a journey of continuous self-improvement, fueled by a willingness to face challenges and embrace change. It requires stepping out of comfort zones, committing to lifelong learning, and intentionally shaping how we show up in our chosen fields. For me, professional growth became a transformative process of redefining my capabilities and building a career that aligned with my purpose.

The first step in professional growth often involves leaving behind what feels safe and familiar. Growth happens when we challenge ourselves to rise to new demands, face unfamiliar situations, and trust in our ability to learn along the way. For me, stepping out of my comfort zone meant saying "yes" to opportunities that seemed discouraging, whether it was taking on leadership roles, navigating uncharted professional environments, or engaging with audiences and colleagues who didn't share my background or perspective.

I learned that growth requires calculated risks. It means applying for positions that stretch your capabilities, speaking up in spaces where your voice feels small, and pursuing projects that seem beyond your reach. These moments of discomfort were pivotal— they taught me resilience, problem-solving, and the value of persistence. Every step into the unknown expanded my perspective and revealed strengths I didn't know I had.

In today's fast-paced world, professional growth demands a commitment to lifelong learning. The skills and knowledge that serve us today may not be enough to meet the challenges of tomorrow. Recognizing this, I made it a priority to seek out opportunities for growth, whether through formal education, certifications, workshops, conferences, research, or self-directed learning.

I also leaned on mentorship as a powerful tool for development. By learning from the experiences of those who had walked the path before me, I gained insights that helped me navigate my own journey more effectively. Mentors not only provided practical advice, but also served as examples of perseverance and success, inspiring me to push past my own limits.

Professional growth also involves staying adaptable. The ability to pivot, embrace new technologies, build partnerships, collaborate, and respond to industry changes is crucial. I learned that adaptability isn't just a skill—it's a mindset. It requires a willingness to unlearn outdated methods, challenge conventional thinking, and remain curious about what's next.

Professional growth enables you to build a personal brand. Acquiring skills or obtaining new career opportunities can be a part of it, but you cannot neglect the advantage of being able to build a personal brand that reflects your values, strengths, and aspirations. Your brand is how you show up in the world—the impression you leave on colleagues, collaborators, and clients.

For me, cultivating a strong personal brand meant developing a reputation of integrity, innovation, creativity, influence, character, care, and a commitment to excellence. I sought to align my professional pursuits with my core values, ensuring that the work I did contributed to a larger purpose and impacted individual's holistic wellness.

Building a personal brand requires intentionality. I had to think about how I communicated my expertise, how I navigated professional spaces, and how I contributed to the goals of the teams and organizations I was part of. By focusing on authenticity, I was able to create meaningful connections and build a legacy that resonated with others.

Professional growth is most rewarding when it aligns with a sense of purpose. For me, this meant pursuing opportunities that allowed me to make an impact, whether by addressing systemic challenges, mentoring others, bridging opportunities gaps, or innovating solutions to complex problems. I was able to use what I gained to inspire others and contribute to a greater good.

Every step of my professional journey reinforced the idea that discomfort is a catalyst for progress. By embracing challenges, committing to learning, and intentionally shaping my professional identity, I discovered the power of growth not only to transform careers, but also to inspire change to live and leave a meaningful legacy.

CRITICAL TRANSITION POINTS

Life is filled with critical transition points, moments that demand adaptation, resilience, perseverance, and a willingness to embrace change. These junctures, often marked by discomfort and uncertainty, are also opportunities for profound transformation, even when the path forward feels unclear.

Transitions such as moving away from home, starting a new job, or facing significant life changes carry a mix of emotions—excitement, fear, anticipation, and hope. For me, one of the most defining transitions came when I left my hometown and stepped into unfamiliar territory. It was a decision filled with apprehension and hesitation, yet it became a turning point that redefined who I was and who I aspired to be. Leaving the familiar behind required me to confront fears, navigate new environments, and discover inner reserves of strength I hadn't known existed. It was in these moments of vulnerability that I began to understand the transformative power of stepping into the unknown.

Pain, while often unwelcome, can serve as a powerful catalyst for growth. One of the most significant moments in my journey was rooted in the pain of loss and disconnection. When I found myself starting over in a new city after losing nearly everything, I felt adrift, isolated from my community, and uncertain of what the future held. What initially seemed like a devastating setback became a fertile ground for purpose to take root. That challenging transition forced me to reevaluate my priorities, realign my goals, and tap into a sense of faith and resilience that carried me through. The pain I experienced ultimately revealed opportunities I couldn't have foreseen and unlocked a deeper understanding of my own capacity for perseverance.

Throughout these transitions, I learned that strength is not found in isolation, but in faith and community. Leaning on others during difficult times became an essential part of my growth. Mentors, friends, and spiritual leaders offered guidance, encouragement, and reassurance when I needed it most. Their support reminded me that growth is not a solitary journey—it is often a collective one. The belief others had in me, especially during moments when I doubted myself, illuminated the importance of surrounding ourselves with people who see our potential and challenge us to rise to it. It was through this interconnectedness that I found the courage to keep moving forward, even when the path was uncertain.

Critical transitions in life may disrupt the familiar and challenge our sense of security, but they also offer us a chance to evolve and redefine ourselves. These moments remind us that while pain and discomfort may shape our experiences, they also have the power to carve out space for growth, resilience, and the discovery of purpose.

GROWTH IS A CHOICE

Growth is a deliberate choice, one that demands intentionality and a willingness to confront discomfort head-on. I came to understand that the challenges I encountered were not merely obstacles meant to hinder me, but opportunities for critical transformation. When I shifted my perspective, I began to view pain as a teacher, adversity as a catalyst, and each struggle as a stepping stone toward a greater sense of purpose and possibility.

The most significant growth often arises from embracing the challenges that life presents. Change, I learned, is embedded in the very fabric of challenge. It requires disrupting familiar patterns, questioning long-held assumptions, and stepping into the unknown. These moments of discomfort, though often challenging, are what push us to stretch beyond our limits and evolve into the best versions of ourselves. Each challenge becomes a crucible, refining us and forging new strengths, even when the process feels overwhelming.

Maintaining a growth mindset in the face of adversity demands both perspective and perseverance. I learned to look beyond the immediate difficulties and focus on the bigger picture, trusting that every struggle was part of a greater plan, even if that plan was not immediately visible. This perspective allowed me to find meaning in hardship and to draw strength from the belief that each obstacle was a necessary part of my journey. Perseverance became my anchor, enabling me to navigate setbacks with resilience and determination, always keeping sight of the potential for growth and transformation that lay ahead.

Choosing growth is not easy, but it is empowering. It requires us to confront discomfort, embrace uncertainty, and trust that the process of change will lead us to a place of greater purpose. By committing to this journey, I discovered that growth is not something that happens to us—it is something we choose, one challenge and one triumph at a time.

MY PERSONAL JOURNEY

One of the most pivotal moments in my journey was the transition from the familiar streets of Chicago to the uncharted territory of DeKalb. At the time, it felt like everything I had known was slipping away. I had lost the stability I clung to, felt disconnected from my community, and was overwhelmed by the uncertainty of what lay ahead. It was a chapter marked by pain, displacement, and a deep sense of loss.

At my lowest point, I sought guidance from a trusted mentor who shared words that would change my perspective: *"Sometimes, we have to leave what is familiar to uncover the path we are truly meant to walk."* Though it didn't lessen the immediate sting of my circumstances, it planted a seed of hope. It reminded me that discomfort and upheaval often precede transformation.

As I began to navigate this unfamiliar chapter of my life, I found myself leaning into faith like never before. I had to trust that this transition, as painful as it was, was leading me toward something greater. With each step, I discovered strengths I didn't realize I possessed—resilience, adaptability, and an openness to new possibilities. I began to see opportunities where there had once been only obstacles and purpose where there had been only pain.

This period of uncertainty ultimately became a catalyst for growth. It forced me to confront my fears, redefine my sense of belonging, and chart a course that was uniquely my own. The challenges I faced shaped my character and deepened my commitment to building a life rooted in faith, purpose, and a vision for the future.

Looking back, I no longer see that moment as a setback. Instead, it stands as a turning point—a moment when the pain of leaving behind what was familiar gave way to the purpose of stepping into something new. That transition taught me that growth often requires us to release what is comfortable and embrace the unknown. Today, I can say with gratitude that the pain of that period was a necessary part of my journey toward fulfillment, meaning, and a life aligned with my greater purpose.

As I reflect on my journey, I see how the choices I made—to lean into discomfort, to persevere when the path was unclear, and to learn from each experience—have shaped me into the person I am today. Growth has allowed me to transform pain into purpose, to inspire others through my story, and to leave a legacy rooted in resilience and hope.

The journey of growth is not one we take alone. It is enriched by the people we encounter, the challenges we overcome, and the lessons we pass on to others. It is a reminder that every step, no matter how small, moves us closer to becoming the person we are meant to be. Growth is not just about what we achieve—it's about who we become along the way. And it is in that becoming that we find the true essence of purpose and fulfillment.

GROWTH IN ACTION

Growth is a continuous journey that requires intention, reflection, and courage to embrace discomfort. The principles shared can guide you in practical ways to step out of your comfort zone and unlock your potential. This hands-on application is designed to help you integrate these principles into your daily life and stay aligned with your growth journey.

1. **Evaluate Your Comfort Zone:** Write down what feels safe and routine in your life. Reflect on what might be holding you back from growth in these areas.

2. **Develop a Growth Mindset:** Replace "I can't" with "I can learn how to." Focus on the potential of what you can achieve with effort and resilience.

3. **Seek Feedback:** Ask a trusted mentor, friend, or colleague for honest input on areas where they believe you could grow and thrive. Use this as an opportunity to gain clarity and perspective.

4. **Celebrate Small Wins:** Recognize and reward yourself for taking even the smallest steps outside your comfort zone. Growth is incremental, and each step is significant.

5. **Identify a Growth Area:** Pinpoint one area of your life—personal and professional—where you feel stagnant or need improvement.

6. **Stretch Goal:** Define a small, but meaningful action that pushes you slightly out of your comfort zone. This could be initiating a challenging conversation, volunteering for a new task, or trying something you've always avoided due to fear or doubt.

GROWTH CHALLENGE

Growth happens when we stretch beyond the boundaries of our comfort zones. To foster a mindset of continuous development, commit to trying one new activity each week that challenges your usual way of thinking or acting. This challenge isn't about achieving perfection—it's about embracing the process of exploration and learning.

Reflect on your experience and journal about the following:

- What made this challenge feel uncomfortable or unfamiliar?
- What did you learn about yourself during this experience?
- How has this challenge changed your perspective or expanded your skills?

_____
_____
_____
_____
_____
_____
_____
_____
_____
_____
_____
_____
_____
_____
_____

4
ADVOCACY

A dvocacy is a powerful act of standing up for what is right, ensuring that your voice and the voices of others are heard. It is about empowerment, self-worth, and building a legacy that extends beyond yourself. My journey with advocacy has been twofold—learning to advocate for myself and using those lessons to fight for others. It has been a transformative path, rooted in the belief that every individual deserves to be valued, respected, and given the opportunity to succeed.

ADVOCATING FOR YOURSELF

Self-advocacy is a skill that's sometimes born out of necessity—a survival mechanism developed in response to feeling unheard, over-looked, or dismissed. For much of my life, I found myself in situations where my voice seemed invisible, where my needs were overshadowed by the priorities of others, and where my value was underestimated. These experiences challenged me in ways that ulti-mately shaped my resilience and self-awareness. They taught me that if I didn't advocate for myself, no one else would.

At school, I often encountered environments where I felt like I didn't belong. As a young person from a marginalized background, I faced both explicit and implicit biases that tested my resolve. Teachers and peers sometimes underestimated my abilities, and I had to push back against stereotypes and assumptions about who I was and what I could achieve. These moments required me to find my voice, to ask for the support I deserved, and to refuse to shrink into the background.

The professional world presented its own set of challenges. In workspaces, I faced instances where my contributions were mini- mized or where I was excluded from opportunities that I had earned. Advocating for myself in these moments meant having the courage to step forward, to ensure that my work was recognized, and to assert my right to equitable treatment. It was not always easy—I encountered moments of psychological unsafety and cultural insen- sitivity that made me hesitate to speak up. But I learned that every time I chose to remain silent, I gave away my power.

Self-advocacy required a mindset shift. I had to unlearn the internalized messages that told me I wasn't worthy of being heard or that speaking up was an act of defiance rather than self-respect. I realized that advocating for myself was not about confrontation or creating conflict. Instead, it was about asserting my humanity, expressing my needs, and setting boundaries that protected my emotional and mental well-being. It meant recognizing my inherent worth and refusing to let others dictate what I deserved.

There were times when I faltered, questioning whether my voice would make a difference or fearing the consequences of speaking out. Would people listen? Would I face retaliation? These fears were real, but each time I chose to advocate for myself, I discovered a new level of strength. I learned that my voice had power, even if it wasn't always met with agreement or immediate change. The act of standing up for myself, regardless of the outcome, was a victory in itself.

Through self-advocacy, I became more skilled at articulating my thoughts, clearly expressing my boundaries, and standing firm in my beliefs. I developed a deeper understanding of my goals and aligned my decisions with them. Whether it was asking for help in a classroom, requesting fair treatment at work, facing inequalities, being a cycle breaker for my family or communicating my needs in personal relationships, each act of advocacy was a step toward reclaiming what was mine.

These moments of courage not only empowered me, but also served as an example for others who might be struggling to find their own voices. By advocating for myself, I demonstrated that it is possible to challenge unfairness and claim your space in any room, no matter how intimidating it may seem. Self-advocacy is a declaration of self-worth—a reminder that we all have the right to be heard, respected, and valued.

ADVOCATING FOR OTHERS

While self-advocacy is essential for personal empowerment, I have always felt a profound responsibility to advocate for others, particularly those from underrepresented and marginalized backgrounds. Advocacy for others goes beyond an act of support; it is a commitment to justice and equity. It is about standing in the gap for those who have been silenced, overlooked, or oppressed and using whatever platform or privilege you have to amplify their voices and their needs.

Advocating for others begins with recognizing the systemic inequities that have shaped their experiences. I've had the privilege of working with students from low-income families, first-generation college attendees, and individuals who face daily battles with systemic barriers. Many of these individuals have incredible potential, but lack the resources, opportunities, or representation needed to thrive. Advocacy, in this context, is not just about identifying those barriers, but actively working to dismantle them and address personal mindsets that align with those barriers.

For me, this work has taken many forms. I have fought to secure scholarships for students who might otherwise be unable to afford higher education, ensuring that their financial circumstances didn't limit their aspirations. I have challenged discriminatory practices within institutions, pushing for policy changes that promote inclusion and equity. In meetings and decision-making spaces, I've made it a point to speak up for those whose voices are often excluded, ensuring that their perspectives and needs are considered.

One of the most rewarding aspects of this advocacy has been working directly with students and mentees to guide them through academic and personal challenges. Advocacy can't be minimized to just fighting battles on someone else's behalf—it's about walking alongside them, offering mentorship, coaching, guidance, and helping them navigate the obstacles in their path deeply rooted. It's about showing them that they are not alone, that they belong, and that they have the power to overcome the odds stacked against them.

Advocacy also involves creating opportunities where none previously existed. For example, I've worked to establish programs and initiatives that provide resources and support for underrepresented students. These efforts go beyond addressing immediate needs—they aim to build systems that uplift entire communities and create pathways for sustained holistic success. Advocacy is an ongoing commitment to building bridges and breaking down barriers.

Perhaps the most fulfilling part of this journey has been witnessing the transformation that occurs when people realize their own power. The focal point of advocacy is not dependence— the primary objective is to foster and promote independence. By equipping others with the tools, knowledge, and confidence to advocate for themselves, we create a lasting effect of empowerment. When people find their voices and learn to speak up for their rights and aspirations, they become agents of change in their own lives and communities.

I've seen this heightened effect in action. A student who once doubted their ability to succeed becomes a leader, advocating for their peers and pushing for changes that benefit future generations. A mentee who hesitated to share their story now uses their experiences to inspire others. These moments reinforce the importance of advocacy as a means of creating lasting impact.

Advocating for others is a privilege. It is a way to honor the struggles of those who came before us and to pave the way for those who will come after. Advocacy ensures that no one is left behind, that everyone has an opportunity to rise, and that the legacy we live and leave is one of inclusion, inspiration, empowerment, excellence, and justice.

GIVING OTHERS A VOICE

Advocacy transcends addressing immediate needs; it challenges and transforms the systems that perpetuate inequality and injustice. To give others a voice means not only speaking up on their behalf, but also creating spaces where they can share their experiences and aspirations. It requires standing alongside individuals and communities, listening with empathy, and taking decisive action to promote equity and community of care. It's about empowering others to join in the fight for justice by first shifting their perspective to an asset based approach to success.

Throughout my work, I have seen the transformative power of collective advocacy. When people unite around a shared cause, their voices amplify each other, creating a force that cannot be ignored. Advocacy is not the work of a single individual—it thrives on collaboration and solidarity. Whether it's rallying for changes in institutional policies, pushing for equal access to education, or demanding accountability in social systems, collective advocacy has shown me that even the most entrenched inequities can be dismantled when people come together with a common purpose.

Giving others a voice begins with listening. True advocacy requires understanding the lived experiences of those you are fighting for. It's about hearing their stories, recognizing their struggles, and validating their emotions. This active listening builds trust and ensures that the solutions being pursued are rooted in the realities of the people most affected. It is a practice of humility and a reminder that advocacy is not about imposing your perspective, but about amplifying the voices of those with lived experiences. It means elevating their stories and ensuring that they are heard and valued.

Transforming systems requires persistence, resilience, and a willingness to challenge the status quo. Advocacy has taught me that change is often slow and fraught with resistance, but it is also deeply rewarding. Each step forward, no matter how small, is a victory for those who have been silenced or ignored. By championing the rights of others and amplifying their voices, we create a world where everyone has the opportunity to thrive.

FIGHTING FOR OPPORTUNITIES

Creating opportunities for others is one of the most effective ways to advocate. For individuals from marginalized backgrounds, access to education, mentorship, experiences, and essential resources is often the key to breaking cycles of inequality and opening doors to a brighter future. Recognizing this, I have made it my mission to fight tirelessly for equitable access to these opportunities, knowing that they serve as the foundation for meaningful change.

Advocacy in this context often means challenging established policies, procedures, and practices that limit access to critical resources. These barriers are not always overt; they are often woven into the fabric of institutions and societal norms, manifesting as funding disparities, biases in decision-making, or inequitable representation in leadership roles. Confronting these obstacles requires persistence, creativity, and an unwavering commitment to justice. It involves asking hard questions, holding systems and people accountable, and refusing to accept the status quo.

One of the most rewarding aspects of advocacy is witnessing the cause-and-effect that opportunities can create. When a student from a low-income background receives a scholarship, they gain more than financial support—they gain hope, confidence, and the belief that they are capable of achieving their dreams. When an organization implements diversity initiatives, it not only transforms the lives of those it uplifts, but also enriches the institution by bringing in and maintain diverse perspectives and talents. These moments of progress remind me why the fight for equitable opportunities is so vital.

Fighting for opportunities also means advocating for systemic change at a macro level. This could involve pushing for better funding in education, ensuring that underserved communities have access to the same quality of resources as more affluent ones. It might mean addressing biases within institutions, from hiring practices that overlook qualified candidates from diverse backgrounds to curricula that fail to reflect the experiences of marginalized groups. Advocacy in these areas demands both tenacity and vision—it requires imagining a world that prioritizes equity and working to make that vision a reality.

On a personal level, my advocacy efforts have involved helping individuals navigate the barriers they face, whether by guiding students through the financial aid process, connecting professionals with mentors who understand their challenges, or pushing for programs that support first-generation college students. These efforts are about more than removing barriers—they are about creating pathways. It's about ensuring that when one door closes, another one opens, and that those who have been historically excluded are not just included, but empowered to thrive.

Advocacy also means cultivating environments where opportunity is not just available, but accessible. This involves challenging assumptions, dismantling stereotypes, and fostering a culture that values diversity, equity, and inclusion. It's about creating systems where everyone has a fair shot, regardless of their background. This kind of advocacy demands courage, as it often involves challenging those in power and confronting uncomfortable truths. But it is also deeply rewarding, as it lays the groundwork for a more just and inclusive society.

In fighting for opportunities, I have learned that progress is not always immediate. The systems we are working to change are often deeply rooted, and the path to equity can be slow and frustrating. Yet, every step forward, no matter how small, is a victory for those who stand to benefit. Advocacy is about the long game— planting seeds of change and nurturing them until they take root and flourish.

Ultimately, fighting for opportunities is about hope. It's about believing in the potential of every individual and working to ensure they have the tools and support they need to succeed. By advocating for equitable access to opportunities, we create a legacy that goes beyond our own lives, touching generations to come and building a world that is more just, compassionate, and inclusive.

THE LEGACY OF ADVOCACY

Advocacy is a cornerstone of building a legacy; it's about creating a foundation for others to rise, ensuring that the obstacles and struggles we faced are not perpetuated for the next generation. Advocacy transforms individual action into collective progress, fostering resilience, hope, and systemic change that reverberates through communities and across generations.

This legacy of advocacy is not defined solely by personal triumphs, but by the lasting impact we make on others and on the structures that shape society. Every act of advocacy, no matter how small, contributes to a larger narrative of progress. Whether it is challenging systemic inequities, empowering underrepresented voices, or fighting for equitable access to opportunities, advocacy becomes a powerful vehicle for transformation. It turns moments of hardship into catalysts for growth and justice, ensuring that the lessons we learn and the battles we fight are not in vain.

A legacy built on advocacy is rooted in the belief that our experiences, no matter how difficult, have value—not only for ourselves, but for others who may walk a similar path. Advocacy allows us to honor those experiences while using them to pave the way for those who come after us. It is a reminder that our struggles can have meaning beyond our own lives, serving as a source of strength and inspiration for future generations.

To leave a legacy of advocacy is to create change that outlasts our time on this earth. It is about challenging the status quo, breaking cycles, and building systems of access. This legacy acknowledges the interconnectedness of our lives and the collective responsibility we share to uplift one another. When we advocate for fairness, dignity, and opportunity, we are shaping the present and creating a vision for a better future.

The power of advocacy lies in its ability to transform lives and inspire others to take up the mantle of change. It shows that one voice, when joined with others, can create a chorus of hope. This collective action has the potential to dismantle systems of oppression, build bridges across divides, and foster a world where everyone has the opportunity to succeed.

Ultimately, the legacy of advocacy is a testament to the enduring power of our voices and our commitment to justice. It is a call to action, reminding us that we have the ability to make a difference and the responsibility to use that ability for good. Through advocacy, we leave behind a roadmap for others to follow, ensuring that the struggles of today give rise to the progress of tomorrow. This is the ultimate purpose of advocacy: to leave the world better than we found it and to inspire others to carry the torch of change forward.

ADVOCACY IN ACTION

Advocacy is about speaking up, challenging inequities, and creating opportunities for yourself and others. It is a call to action to use your voice, your resources, and your influence to make a difference. Self-advocacy is about identifying your needs and learning how to advocate for them, which requires self-reflection. Often, we lose ourselves while focusing on the needs of others. This applicational section will help you identify practical ways to incorporate self-advocacy into your daily life and inspire you to become an agent of C.H.A.N.G.E.™

1. **Identify Areas of Need for Self-Advocacy:** Think about issues or communities that resonate with you. Advocacy starts with passion. It might be related to education, equality, mental health, or social justice. Choose something meaningful to you.

2. **Use Your Skills to Serve Others:** Identify the talents, knowledge, or resources you possess and how they can benefit others. For instance, if you're a writer, help someone draft a résumé or a petition. If you're in education, mentor a student or volunteer your time.

3. **Create Opportunities:** Advocate for inclusion by recommending someone for a role, sharing an opportunity with someone who might not have access to it, or helping someone network in your field. She resources with others

4. **Learn About Systems and Policies:** Advocacy requires understanding the structures you aim to influence. Research policies, community needs, or the challenges faced by the people you wish to help. Knowledge equips you to advocate effectively.

ADVOCACY CHALLENGE

Advocacy begins with action, and often the most impactful actions start close to home. This challenge invites you to take a deliberate step in supporting someone who may need your help to be seen, heard, or uplifted. By amplifying their voice, you not only empower them, but also cultivate your ability to create meaningful change.

1. Take a moment to think about someone in your life who might benefit from your support. This could be a colleague navigating challenges at work, a friend pursuing a goal, but lacking confidence, or a member of your community facing systemic barriers.

2. Consider their situation, their needs, and the obstacles they might be facing.

3. Approach the person with genuine empathy and curiosity. Ask open-ended questions to understand how you can help.

4. Listen attentively to their response, and respect their boundaries. Advocacy is about collaboration, not assumption.

5. Based on their expressed needs, take one concrete step to amplify their voice or provide tangible support.

Reflect on your experience and journal about the following:

- How did it feel to intentionally advocate for someone else or even yourself?
- How did your advocacy make a difference for the person you supported?
- What did you learn about the power of your voice and actions?
- How can you continue to create opportunities to support and amplify your voice in the future?

5
COMMUNITY

Community is often a lifeline for many. It's a structure and a force that helps to shape lives in a myriad of ways. In my journey, I came to realize the truth of the old adage: *It takes a village.* It takes a community to build what you didn't have, to fill in the gaps left by circumstances, and to foster growth where isolation once reigned. Community is about more than just physical proximity; it's about shared purpose, mutual support, and collective empowerment.

THE IMPORTANCE OF HAVING A COMMUNITY

A strong community is the foundation of both personal and collective growth. It provides more than just a group of people to interact with—it creates a network of belonging, understanding, and shared purpose. Within a community, individuals find not only support, but also encouragement to strive for their goals and overcome obstacles. It is in the moments of uncertainty, adversity, or even triumph that the presence of a community proves invaluable.

The strength of a community lies in its ability to lift you up when you falter, to celebrate your successes as if they were their own, and to remind you that you are never alone in your journey by being present. Whether it's family, friends, mentors, or colleagues, the people who form your community are the ones who provide a safety net when life feels overwhelming. They are the voices that reassure you, the hands that help you rise, and the hearts that root for your success, but you have to find people that you trust and can be vulnerable with.

For me, the concept of community became especially significant during periods of transition and growth. Life's challenges have a way of isolating you, making you feel as though you have to navigate uncharted waters alone. It was during these moments that I truly understood the power of having a supportive network. My community not only provided the guidance and resources I needed, but also gave me the courage to continue moving forward when self-doubt crept in.

Community offers fresh perspectives that you may not have considered. When you're immersed in your own challenges, it's easy to feel stuck or to lose sight of the bigger picture. A strong community provides clarity by sharing wisdom and insight that can illuminate a path forward. Whether it's a mentor offering practical advice, a friend lending an empathetic ear, or a peer challenging you to see things differently, these interactions create opportunities for growth.

Resilience is another gift that comes from being part of a community. The collective strength of people who believe in you helps you to weather storms that might otherwise seem insurmountable. It's not just about the support you receive; it's about the knowledge that others have faced and overcome similar struggles. Their stories of perseverance inspire your own, reinforcing the belief that you, too, can endure and thrive.

In my journey, I learned that a community is not just beneficial—it is essential. Life was never meant to be a solitary endeavor, and growth is seldom achieved in isolation. Through the shared connections of a community, we find the courage to dream bigger, the strength to overcome challenges, and the wisdom to navigate our paths with purpose. A community doesn't just help you survive—it helps you flourish.

COMMUNITY BUILDING AND ITS EFFECTS

Building a community is an intentional and purposeful act. It requires time, trust, and a genuine willingness to invest in relationships. At its core, community building is about creating connections that uplift, inspire, and provide mutual support. These connections don't just serve the individuals within the group—they ripple outward, empowering entire communities and creating a foundation for collective success.

When nurtured, communities have an extraordinary impact. They amplify individual strengths, foster collective resilience, and create opportunities that might otherwise remain out of reach. A well-built community becomes a source of encouragement, a platform for collaboration, and a catalyst for growth. It's where people feel seen, valued, and supported, which, in turn, motivates them to give back and contribute to the well-being of others.

In my own journey, I experienced the transformative power of community building firsthand. Engaging with others, sharing knowledge, and working toward common goals not only enriched my life, but also reinforced my sense of purpose. I saw how a simple act of connection could inspire profound change. Whether it was mentoring students, collaborating with peers, or joining forces with like-minded individuals, these relationships became the foundation for progress and growth.

One of the most profound effects of community building is the sense of unity it fosters. When people come together with shared goals and mutual respect, they create something larger than themselves. This unity not only strengthens bonds, but also encourages individuals to stretch beyond their limits. Challenges that might feel insurmountable alone become manageable when faced together, and victories are more meaningful when shared.

Community building also creates a space where innovation thrives. When diverse perspectives come together, they generate ideas and solutions that would be difficult to achieve in isolation. The exchange of knowledge, skills, and experiences fuels creativity and leads to breakthroughs that benefit everyone involved.

For me, community became a source of fulfillment and a reminder of the power of collaboration. Each relationship built, each connection nurtured, contributed to a larger vision of empowerment and success. Community building taught me that we are stronger together, that our collective resilience can overcome even the greatest challenges, and that the act of creating connections is, in itself, an act of hope and purpose.

A well-built community doesn't just impact those within it; it leaves a legacy. It becomes a living testament to the power of relationships and the profound changes that can occur when people come together with intention and purpose. Through community, we find not only the strength to grow, but also the ability to create a lasting impact that transcends individual efforts.

A LACK OF COMMUNITY AND ITS IMPACT

Early in life, the absence of a supportive community left a deep-rooted mark on me. Growing up without the safety net of a village meant I often faced life's challenges feeling isolated and detached. I lacked the guidance that mentors, peers, and extended networks can provide, leaving me unsure of how to navigate the complexities of life. Without access to a community that could offer wisdom, encouragement, or resources, I found myself piecing together solutions on my own, often through trial and error.

This absence was not just a practical gap—it was an emotional one as well. Without a community to uplift and validate my experiences, I often questioned my own worth and potential. The sense of isolation fostered self-doubt and made the road to self-discovery and growth feel infinitely steeper. Challenges that might have been easier with support felt insurmountable, and successes often went unacknowledged.

However, the lack of community also served as a powerful teacher. It underscored for me the vital role that connection plays in growth and resilience. I came to understand that thriving requires more than personal determination—it requires a network of people who believe in you, who challenge you to be better, and who walk beside you on the journey.

As I grew older, I realized that if I didn't have a village, I would have to build one intentionally. I sought out mentors, peers, and allies who shared my values and aspirations. I surrounded myself with people who not only saw my potential, but also encouraged me to pursue it. This process of creating my own community was not easy—it required vulnerability, effort, and the courage to reach out —but it became a transformative force in my life.

Building my own village allowed me to heal from the wounds of isolation. It provided the affirmation and support I needed to grow and redefine my path. I discovered that community is not just about proximity or shared experiences—it's about shared purpose and mutual care. My self-made community became a foundation for strength, enabling me to overcome obstacles and embrace opportunities I once thought were beyond my reach.

The impact of that early absence of community is something I carry with me even now. It drives my commitment to fostering connection, both for myself and for others. I understand deeply how the lack of a village can limit one's sense of possibility, and I am dedicated to ensuring that others don't have to face those same struggles alone. Building and nurturing community has not only been a transformative experience for me, but also a way to pay forward the lessons I've learned and the strength I've gained.

COMMUNITIES CREATE OPPORTUNITIES

Intentionality is the foundation of building meaningful and impactful communities. A thriving community doesn't just happen by chance; it requires deliberate effort, a clear vision, and active engagement. Hoping for connections or waiting for them to naturally develop isn't enough—you have to seek them out, nurture them, and contribute to their growth.

For me, creating intentional communities involved stepping out of my comfort zone. It meant attending events where I knew no one, initiating conversations that felt intimidating, and seeking out individuals who shared my values, aspirations, and vision. These were not always easy steps, but they were necessary to surround myself with people who could inspire, guide, and support me on my journey.

These intentional communities became lifelines in ways I couldn't have imagined. They provided mentorship that challenged me to grow, resources that opened doors, and support that carried me through challenging times. They were places where my ideas were validated, my voice was heard, and my potential was nurtured. Each connection I made reinforced the importance of community and reminded me that no one succeeds in isolation.

From professional organizations to faith-based groups, each intentional community played a unique role in my development. Professional organizations gave me access to expertise, networking opportunities, and tools to enhance my career. Faith-based groups, on the other hand, offered emotional and spiritual support, reminding me of the power of shared values and collective purpose. Social networks provided camaraderie, encouragement, and inspiration, making every success feel shared and every setback more bearable.

What I found most powerful about intentional communities was their capacity to create opportunities. Through collaboration and mutual support, these communities became ecosystems of growth and possibility. They allowed me to tap into resources I wouldn't have discovered on my own, and they opened doors I hadn't even known existed.

Being part of intentional communities also taught me the value of giving back. These weren't just spaces where I sought help or guidance—they were spaces where I contributed, supported others, and played an active role in fostering growth for everyone involved. By giving as much as I received, I experienced the true spirit of community and the exponential power it has to uplift individuals and transform lives.

Through intentionality, I learned that community is a dynamic, reciprocal force. It's great to find people who align with your vision, but it's also important to invest in relationships that create collective success. Each connection, each act of support, and each collaboration built a network that not only bolstered my journey, but also became a source of strength, opportunity, and transformation for others. Intentional communities, I realized, are more than just groups of people—they are engines of possibility that propel us toward a brighter future.

EFFECTS OF MENTORSHIP

The presence of mentors in my life has been life-changing— offering guidance, perspective, and unwavering belief in my potential, especially during moments when I struggled to see it myself. Their support often served as a lifeline, helping me navigate challenges, clarify my goals, and find the courage to step into my purpose.

Mentors can be critical for personal transitions in your life. You may be grappling with uncertainty, unsure of your next steps, orr burdened by self-doubt. Mentors can offer you more than just advice — they can listen deeply, validate your feelings, and gently challenge you to think bigger. Many will opt to share their own experiences of overcoming obstacles— therefore, reminding you that growth often comes from discomfort and that resilience is built in the face of adversity. Their belief in you can rekindle your confidence and push you to pursue opportunities you had once dismissed as unattainable.

Mentors can also be essential for professional development, teaching you the importance of strategic thinking and intentionality in your work. Mentors model leadership that is grounded in empathy and purpose, demonstrating that success isn't just about individual achievement—it's about lifting others along the way. Through their professional mentorship, you can learn how to navigate complex systems, advocate for yourself and others, and approach challenges with both courage and humility.

As a result of being mentored, I have embraced opportunities to mentor others, paying forward the invaluable support I received. Mentorship, I've discovered, is a reciprocal relationship—a two-way street of giving and receiving, teaching and learning. Each time I mentor someone, I am reminded of the power of shared experiences and the importance of seeing and nurturing potential in others.

One of the most rewarding aspects of mentorship is witnessing the growth and success of those I've had the privilege to guide. Whether it's helping a student navigate the intricacies of higher education, supporting a colleague through a career transition, or offering encouragement to someone facing personal challenges, these moments of connection reaffirm the value of mentorship.

Through mentoring, I have also deepened my understanding of leadership and empathy. It has taught me to listen with intention, to meet people where they are, and to create spaces where others feel seen, heard, and valued. Mentorship has shown me that growth is a collective journey and that by sharing our stories and insights, we can inspire transformation not only in others, but also in ourselves.

The relationships built through mentorship have been some of the most meaningful in my life. They have reinforced the idea that community is not just about the connections we make, but also about the ways we invest in each other's growth. By being both a mentee and a mentor, I have experienced the beauty of mentorship as a living, evolving bond—one that shapes lives, creates opportunities, and fosters a legacy of empowerment and shared success.

GIVING BACK STRENGTHENS YOUR FOUNDATION

Giving back to your community is more than an act of kindness—it's a fundamental way to fortify the connections that shape who you are. It creates a cycle of empowerment, where the support you provide to others also reinforces your own foundation. When you give back, you don't just contribute to the well-being of others; you invest in the collective strength, resilience, and potential of your community.

For me, giving back has been transformative. It is an expression of gratitude for the guidance and opportunities I've received and a commitment to ensuring that others have access to the same, if not greater, resources and support. Whether through mentoring students, volunteering at community events, or advocating for systemic change, giving back has allowed me to deepen my connection to the people and places that have shaped my journey.

One of the most powerful aspects of giving back is its ability to foster resilience—not just in individuals, but across entire communities. When you step into the role of mentor, advocate, or supporter, you help others see their own strength and potential. You also remind yourself of the progress you've made and the importance of creating a legacy that lifts others.

Through my work, I've witnessed firsthand how giving back builds trust and opens doors for collaboration and growth. Each time I've taken the time to support someone—whether by helping them navigate a challenge, offering encouragement, or sharing resources—I've seen how those moments of connection plant seeds of hope and transformation.

Giving back is also a way to honor the support you've received. It's a way of saying, "I see you, and I want to help you succeed because someone once did the same for me." This mindset reinforces the idea that success is not meant to be hoarded, but shared. It's about recognizing that our achievements are often the result of collective effort and that by lifting others, we strengthen the foundation we all stand on.

In giving back, I've found purpose and fulfillment that goes beyond personal achievement. It has reminded me of the power of community, the importance of collaboration, and the joy of seeing others thrive. By investing in others, we create a legacy rooted in resilience, hope, and shared growth.

When we give back, we become part of something greater than ourselves. We ensure that the connections we build, the lessons we've learned, and the support we've received continue to shape lives for generations to come. It is through giving that we truly solidify our foundation, not just as individuals, but as members of a vibrant, interconnected community.

COMMUNAL STRENGTH

While it takes a village to build what you didn't have, it also takes intention, trust, and effort to create and sustain that village. In my journey, community has been a constant reminder that we are never truly alone. It has taught me that every effort to build connections, however small, contributes to a larger foundation of shared strength and purpose.

Through the communities I've been part of—and the ones I've had the privilege to help create—I have seen firsthand how collaboration can amplify success, how mutual support can spark transformation, and how belonging can inspire courage. We must acknowledge that while we are all on our unique paths, the journey becomes richer, more fulfilling, and more impactful when we walk it together.

Community reminds us that we don't have to have all the answers or carry all the weight on our own. It shows us that by leaning on others and allowing them to lean on us, we create a cycle of empowerment that benefits everyone involved. It is in these moments of connection that we find the courage to dream bigger, to take risks, and to imagine a future brighter than we ever thought possible.

The work of building a community—a village— is ongoing, but the rewards are immeasurable. Every relationship, every act of support, every moment of shared purpose strengthens the foundation of community. It truly takes a village to create lasting growth, and the village is worth every ounce of effort. In the end, community is not just something we are part of—it is something we create, nurture, and carry forward, ensuring its impact resonates for generations to come.

COMMUNITY IN ACTION

Community is the foundation for collaboration, support, and shared growth. Living out the principles of community means creating and nurturing connections that uplift and empower everyone involved. By fostering intentional relationships and cultivating a sense of unity, you can build a supportive network that inspires collective success.

1. **Identify Your Existing Communities:** Reflect on the groups, networks, or relationships you are already part of. This might include family, work colleagues, faith-based organizations, or social clubs. If you do not have it, consider taking the steps to identify people in those areas. Recognize the value they bring and where they may need strengthening.

2. **Reach Out Intentionally:** Start with one action to deepen a connection or forge a new one. Whether it's sending a thoughtful message, inviting someone for coffee, lunch, or attending a local event, these small steps can lead to meaningful relationships.

3. **Contribute to the Community:** Offer your time, skills, or resources to a community effort. This could include volunteering, mentoring someone within the group, or participating in a collaborative project. Contribution fosters belonging and demonstrates leadership.

4. **Build a Community of Care:** Surround yourself with people who encourage growth and provide mutual support. Seek connections that align with your values and create spaces where psychological safety, trust, and empathy are prioritized.

5. **Celebrate Collective Wins:** Recognize and celebrate the accomplishments of your community. Whether it's sharing successes on social media, organizing a group

celebration, simply expressing gratitude, or being present to support. Celebrating together strengthens bonds.

COMMUNITY CHALLENGE

Fostering meaningful connections requires intentionality. For this challenge, start a "Connection Project" that focuses on strengthening relationships and creating opportunities for collaboration and networking. Here's how:

Step 1: Choose Three People to Connect With

Think about people in different areas of your life—professional, personal, or social. This could include a mentor, a family member, or someone you've always admired, but haven't reached out to yet.

Step 2: Plan an Intentional Interaction

Decide how you will connect. This could be:

- A heartfelt email expressing your appreciation
- A phone call to catch up and asking how you can support
- Scheduling time for coffee or lunch to build a deeper connection

Step 3: Follow Up with Gratitude

After your interaction, express gratitude for their time and the value they bring to your life. This reinforces the connection and sets the stage for future interactions.

Reflect on your experience and journal about the following:

- How did connecting with others impact your sense of community and belonging?
- What did you learn from the people you reached out to?
- How can you maintain and nurture these relationships over time?

_____
_____
_____
_____
_____
_____
_____
_____
_____
_____
_____
_____
_____
_____
_____
_____
_____
_____
_____
_____
_____
_____
_____
_____

6

YIELDING

Yielding is an act of surrender, a conscious decision to trust in something greater than ourselves. For me, it has been a journey of faith—trusting God's plan when the road ahead was unclear and my own instincts pushed me to maintain control. Yielding isn't just about giving up; it's about giving in to the processes, guidance, and lessons meant to shape us.It's a true blessing to find people you can trust and be vulnerable with—those who offer a space of psychological safety. For me, that sense of safety came through my faith, especially during a time in my life when I was the one others relied on, yet didn't have the same support in return.

Faith has been the cornerstone of my success, the foundation upon which I've built my resilience, my growth, and my purpose. It's the quiet assurance that even when life feels uncertain, there is a plan unfolding—a plan greater than anything I could have designed for myself. This has kept me anchored, and has been my inspiration to keep going during the times I wanted to give up.

FAITH AS THE FOUNDATION

Faith has always been more than a passive belief for me—it has been the very structure that holds everything together.

> *I didn't need to figure it out.*
> *I didn't need to determine how things would be.*
> *I just needed to surrender.*
> *I just needed to have faith.*
> *I just needed to believe.*
> *I just needed to trust in God's plan and align myself with*
>   *His purpose for my life.*

Like a cornerstone in a building, faith supports the weight of my aspirations, dreams, and challenges. It is the unshakable base that provides stability when life feels uncertain or overwhelming. Without faith as my foundation, my life would feel unstable, unable to withstand the pressures of life changes, disappointment, grief, and the unknown.

What makes faith so essential is its transformative power. It doesn't remove life's challenges or guarantee easy solutions, but it provides a lens through which I can see hope in the midst of trials. Faith gives purpose to struggles, making them stepping stones instead of stumbling blocks. It is the reminder that even in the darkest moments, I am never alone and that there is a greater plan at work.

Yet, yielding to faith doesn't come naturally—it requires trust in a plan that is often invisible and beyond my comprehension. Letting go of the need to control outcomes is one of the hardest lessons I've had to learn. Like many, I've faced the fear of the unknown and the anxiety that comes with not knowing what's next. Faith, however, calls us to step forward, even when we can't see the entire path. It's a conscious decision to release the tight grip of fear and lean into trust.

I've learned that faith is not the absence of doubt. Doubt is natural—it creeps in when the journey is hard, the answers are delayed, or the circumstances seem overwhelming. But faith is the willingness to move forward despite that doubt. It's a daily practice of surrendering the illusion of control and choosing to believe that what is unseen is still real and what is uncertain is still guided.

Faith as my foundation has given me the strength to navigate life's complexities with a sense of peace and resilience. It has taught me that even when I don't have all the answers, I can trust that the structure built on faith will hold. It allows me to dream boldly, face challenges with courage, and embrace the unknown with hope. It reminds me that the foundation of faith is not just about holding things together—it's about building something extraordinary, one step of trust at a time.

LETTING GO AND TRUSTING THE PROCESS

Surrendering control can be a challenge. As humans, we naturally cling to our plans, desires, and expectations. We map out our futures with precision, holding tightly to the belief that control will guarantee success or shield us from pain. Letting go feels counterintuitive, like relinquishing our power, but I've learned that surrendering to the process— is where true freedom and transformation begin.

Perhaps there are moments when surrendering feels impossible. When life's challenges are intense, and outcomes seem unattainable, it's easy to struggle with the fear of losing control. Your mind may be consumed by "what-ifs," and cling to the false security of your own understanding. Yet, in those moments, faith can become your anchor, gently nudging you to yield. Yielding doesn't mean abandoning effort or passively waiting for change; it means trusting the process, even when you can't see the path forward.

Yielding requires stepping out of your comfort zone and releasing your grip on the outcomes you worked so hard to orchestrate. Being open to the guidance and insight that you may seek out through consulting, counseling, coaching, mentorship, faith, and/or from peers. Its's not easy. There may be times when doubt whispers that letting go might lead to failure, disappointment, or worse—a loss of identity. Yet, every time I loosened my grip, I discovered that what I gained was far greater than what I thought I was giving up. Faith is truly transformative when you release control and surrender to becoming vulnerable enough to trust.

Surrendering is not about giving up because defeat is not an option; it's about giving way. Surrendering doesn't signify weakness or defeat. It creates space for— divine guidance to take root, growth that couldn't happen within the confines of our own plans, and unexpected blessings.

In the act of letting go, I came to understand that challenges aren't without purpose. They are opportunities for transformation— teaching resilience, fostering patience, and bringing to surface the areas of change needed in our lives to thrive. Trusting the process has shown me that even when life feels out of control, there is a greater plan at work—one that is unfolding for my good, even if I can't yet see the full picture. This is where trusting the process is implemented.

Surrendering control taught me to let go of the illusion that I needed to have everything figured out. It freed me from the anxiety of not being enough based on society's standards and reminded me to lean in to my purpose. I learned that true power lies not in forcing outcomes, but in trusting the journey and embracing the growth it brings. Through surrender, I found peace in the uncertainty and strength in knowing I was never navigating it alone even in time of abandonment or rejection.

A STORY OF SURRENDER AND BLESSINGS

There was a pivotal moment in my life when I had no choice, but to yield completely—to surrender my fears, my plans, and my expectations. It happened when I transitioned from Chicago to DeKalb, leaving behind everything familiar to step into the unknown. At that time, I felt as though my life had unraveled. I had lost almost everything, and the prospect of starting over in an unfamiliar place was overwhelming. The weight of doubt and fear pressed heavily on me, and I questioned whether I was making the right decision.

Yet, in the midst of that uncertainty, a quiet voice of faith began to speak. It reminded me that this moment of upheaval wasn't the end—it was the beginning of something greater. I leaned deeply into Scripture, especially Proverbs 3:5-6: "Trust in the Lord with all your heart and lean not on your own understanding; in all your ways submit to Him, and He will make your paths straight." Those words became my lifeline, a constant reassurance that even though I couldn't see the road ahead, God was guiding me.

Surrendering to this process was one of the hardest things I've ever done. I had to let go of the life I had built in Chicago, the comfort of familiarity, and the illusion that I had reached the best version of myself. I had to trust that moving to DeKalb, a place where I felt like a stranger, was part of a divine plan. At times, the doubts would creep in: Was this really what God wanted for me? Would I be able to rebuild my life in this new environment? But each time fear tried to take hold, I reminded myself to yield and trust the process of the unknown.

The blessings that came from this act of surrender were beyond anything I could have envisioned. In DeKalb, I discovered opportunities that aligned with my purpose in ways I hadn't imagined. Professionally, I was given platforms to lead and grow, to use my skills in meaningful ways that positively impacted others. Personally, I experienced an incredible sense of renewal—a rebuilding of not just my circumstances, but also my spirit. It guided me down a path of holistic success.

What I initially saw as a loss became a season of favor. The relationships I formed, the lessons I learned, and the milestones I achieved in DeKalb were not just coincidental—they were evidence of a plan far greater than my own. It was as if every moment of uncertainty in my journey had been preparing me for the blessings that awaited.

This story of surrender taught me that yielding isn't about giving up—it's about giving in to something greater. It's about trusting that even when life feels chaotic, there is a divine purpose unfolding. My time in DeKalb became a testimony of faith, resilience, grit, perseverance, and triumph. What felt like a step into darkness was, in truth, a step into light—a season of growth, favor, and purpose that I will forever be grateful for. I became a trailblazer and champion who turned adversity into achievements; I am an overcomer.

YIELDING AND HOLISTIC SUCCESS

Yielding is not solely about faith; it encompasses a mindset that embraces balance and wholeness, allowing for holistic success. True success goes far beyond career achievements or financial stability—it's about cultivating harmony across every dimension of life: spiritual, emotional, relational, and physical. Holistic success is rooted in the belief that each area of life feeds into and strengthens the others, creating a life that is both meaningful and sustainable.

Yielding involves letting go of the singular focus on excelling in one domain at the expense of others. It means resisting the societal pressures that equate success with constant hustle and instead pursuing wholeness. Yielding asks us to trust that, in time, all the pieces of our lives will align, and that the journey toward balance is as significant as any milestone we may achieve.

For me, yielding has been an intentional practice of surrendering the urge to prove I was worthy of love, care, and support to focusing on nurturing my overall well-being. It meant leaning into holistic wellness—not as an indulgence, but as a necessity for sustained growth and resilience. I've learned to honor moments of stillness, where I can pause, reflect, and recalibrate, allowing myself to reconnect with the deeper purpose behind my efforts. These moments remind me that progress is not always measured by outward accomplishments, but by inner peace and clarity.

Yielding has also required me to trust in processes that foster growth, even when they challenge my patience. It has meant accepting that growth is not always linear and that setbacks often serve as opportunities for reflection and recalibration. By yielding to these processes, I've discovered a strength and resilience I didn't know I had—a capacity to adapt, to heal, and to persevere.

This mindset of yielding encourages presence in the journey, rather than fixation on the destination. It's about finding joy and meaning in the everyday moments, trusting that they are building the foundation for something greater. Yielding has allowed me to release the pressure of societal norms and embrace the idea that success is a mosaic made up of many facets of life, all interwoven and equally important.

Holistic success is an ongoing journey. It's about finding balance in the here and now, while holding faith that the future will unfold as it should. Yielding reminds me that every step of faith, every act of self-care, and every moment of stillness is a step closer to becoming the best version of myself. As a lifelong learner, it's a process of continual trusting, growing, and aligning with the greater purpose that guides my life.

Faithful surrender is the bridge between where we are and where we are destined to be. It connects us to the abundant blessings and profound growth that await on the other side of trust. Faith, as the cornerstone of a life well-lived, reminds us that we are never alone on this journey. And in yielding, we find not only the strength to persevere, but also the grace to thrive.

You are not entitled to anything, but you deserve everything. Your legacy begins now—with the life you live. This book provides the guidance you need to process strategies for success, with me as your professional GPS. Defeat is not an option. By embracing a holistic approach to success, you can unlock your fullest potential, overcome barriers, and rise above systemic oppression to build a life of purpose and impact. Here is legacy unlocked!

YIELDING IN ACTION

Yielding is about surrendering control and trusting the process in times of uncertainty. To implement the principles of yielding in your daily life, you can focus on embracing patience, seeking clarity through reflection, and taking intentional steps while leaving space for growth and discovery. It's important to be teachable when seeking insight and guidance to understand your blindspots. Let go of behaviors, patterns, and people that keep you stagnant. Yielding doesn't mean giving up—it means aligning your actions with purpose.

1. **Start Your Day with Reflection:** Spend 5–10 minutes in meditation, prayer, or quiet reflection. Use this time to align your thoughts, focus on your intentions, and seek guidance for the day ahead.

2. **Practice Patience in Uncertainty:** When faced with challenges or delays, remind yourself to step back, take a deep breath, and trust that the outcome will unfold in its own time after you have done your part.

3. **Write a Gratitude List:** Each evening, list three things you are grateful for, focusing on moments when surrendering led to positive outcomes or clarity.

4. **Embrace Flexibility:** Commit to remaining open to changes in plans or outcomes, seeing them as opportunities for growth rather than setbacks.

YIELDING CHALLENGE

Set aside one full day to practice yielding in every aspect of your life. Begin the day by reflecting on areas where you often feel the need to maintain control. Choose one of these areas and intentionally let go of your expectations. For example, you might refrain from micro-managing a project, allow a loved one to take the lead in decision-making, or trust in the timing of an event without trying to force an outcome.

Throughout the day, focus on staying present and embracing a mindset of surrender. When moments of discomfort or anxiety arise, pause and take three deep breaths, repeating an affirmation such as, "I trust the process, and I am open to what unfolds." End the day with gratitude by journaling about your experience, noting any unexpected blessings, insights, or feelings of relief that emerged from yielding.

Reflect on your experience and journal about the following:

- What did you learn about yourself through the process of surrendering for a day?
- What unexpected outcomes or blessings did you experience by letting go of control?
- How can you incorporate the practice of yielding into your daily routine to create a balanced and peaceful life?

_____
_____
_____
_____
_____
_____
_____
_____

7

THE JOURNEY OF L.E.G.A.C.Y.™

As we come to the conclusion of this journey, let us reflect on the path we've traveled together through pillars of the L.E.G.A.C.Y.™ framework. Leadership, Education, Growth, Advocacy, Community, and Yielding—each pillar represents a powerful tool for building a life of purpose, impact, and transformation. Together, they form a blueprint for not only navigating challenges, but also for thriving in the face of change.

The L.E.G.A.C.Y.™ framework is more than a set of principles; it's a call to action. It reminds us that legacy is not simply what we leave behind, but what we live every day. It's the values we embody, the lives we touch, and the courage we show in embracing our unique journey.

Through the daily application of these pillars, we become living examples of resilience, hope, and determination. We set the standard of excellence in place of perfection to always excel.

Here's a brief review of the framework we explored:

1. Leadership: Leading from Within

Leadership begins with self-awareness and self-leadership. It challenges us to take ownership of our lives, make intentional choices, and influence others through our actions and integrity. By stepping into the role of a leader, we create ripples of change that extend far beyond ourselves.

2. Education: Empowerment Through Knowledge

Education equips us with the tools to navigate life, disrupt limitations, and shape our future. It is a lifelong pursuit that goes beyond formal schooling, encompassing curiosity, mentorship, and the wisdom gained from lived experiences. Education is the foundation for informed decisions and empowered living.

3. Growth: Embracing Discomfort

Growth is a choice that requires courage and resilience. It calls us to step out of our comfort zones, confront our fears, and embrace the transformation that comes through challenges. Each step toward growth strengthens our capacity to become the best version of ourselves. The change is in the challenge.

4. Advocacy: A Voice for Change and Support

Advocacy is the heart of building a legacy that extends beyond individual success. It empowers us to stand up for what is right, fight for those who cannot fight for themselves, and create opportunities for others. Advocacy challenges systems of inequality and amplifies the voices of those who have been silenced. Self-advocacy strengthens your voice to ask for the help you need and empowers you to do the same for others.

5. Community: Building Together

Community reminds us that we are not alone in this journey. It fosters connection, collaboration, and mutual support, providing the foundation for shared growth and impact. A strong community uplifts and empowers, proving that it truly takes a village to build what we need and make change to systemic barriers.

6. Yielding: Trusting the Process

Yielding teaches us the power of surrender and trust. It calls us to let go of control, embrace faith, and open ourselves to guidance and possibilities beyond our understanding. In yielding, we find clarity, peace, and alignment with a greater purpose.

LIVE YOUR L.E.G.A.C.Y.™

Your L.E.G.A.C.Y.™ starts now. There is no perfect moment, no magic milestone—just the choices you make every day. As you continue your journey, remember that your legacy is shaped by how you live, learn, grow, advocate, connect, and trust. The steps you take today not only transform your own life, but also inspire others to dream bigger, reach higher, and persevere through their own challenges.

Legacy is a journey, not a destination. It is found in the small, consistent actions that align with your values and purpose. The pillars of the framework can be utilized at different stages of your life for individuals, business, programs, planning, families, professional development, and meeting continual outcomes. It is built through the lives you touch, the communities you nurture, and the courage you show in the face of adversity. By embracing the L.E.G.A.C.Y.™ framework, you create a life of meaning, impact, and inspiration—a life that stands as a testament to the power of resilience.

As you close this book, take a moment to reflect on your own legacy. What story are you writing? What impact are you creating? And how will you continue to live your L.E.G.A.C.Y.™ each day so it lives on beyond you?

The future is yours to shape.
Your legacy is waiting.
Live it *boldly*, *authentically*, and with *purpose*.

ADDITIONAL RESOURCES

Your journey toward making a *Unique I.M.P.A.C.T.™* doesn't end here. True transformation comes from continuous growth, learning, and connection. In this section, you'll find books, journal articles, websites, theories, and terms/ concepts to help you build on the principles of empowerment, resilience, and community shared throughout this book. These resources are designed to support you as you create lasting change in your life and the lives of those around you. Let's continue this journey—together.

BOOKS/ WEBSITES/ JOURNAL ARTICLES

- Ashley, E. L. (n.d.). Trust the process: Embracing challenges and finding purpose. Retrieved from https://www.ashleyelizabethlynne.com/trust-the-process/

- Balemian, K., & Feng, J. (2013). First generation students: College aspirations, preparedness and challenges. Retrieved from http://research.collegeboard.org/sites/default/filed/publications/2013/8/presentation-apac-2013-first-generation-college-aspirations-preparedness-challenges.pdf

- Bass, B. M., & Avolio, B. J. (1994). Improving organizational effectiveness through transformational leadership. SAGE Publications.

- Bolma, L.G. & Gallos, J.V. (2011). *Reframing Academic Leadership*. San Francisco: Jossey-Bass.

- Bridges, W. (2004). Transitions: Making sense of life's changes (2nd ed.). Da Capo Press.

- Brown, B. (2012). Daring greatly: How the courage to beAshley, E. L. (n.d.). Trust the process: Embracing challenges and finding purpose. Retrieved from https://www.ashleyelizabethlynne.com/trust-the-process/

- Bryant, T. (2023). *Homecoming: Overcome fear and trauma to reclaim your whole authentic self*. HarperOne.

- Capriccioso, R. (2006). Aiding first generation students. *Inside Higher Ed*. Retrieved from http://www.insidehighered.com/news

- Center for Creative Leadership. (n.d.). Leadership styles. Center for Creative Leadership.

- Claro, S., Paunesku, D., & Dweck, C. S. (2016). Growth mindset tempers the effects of poverty on academic achievement. Proceedings of the National Academy of Sciences, 113(31), 8664–8668. https://doi.org/10.1073/pnas.160820711

- Delman, A. (2021, August 19). Why it's important to embrace uncertainty during transitions. Psychology Today. Retrieved from https://www.psychologytoday.com/us/blog/life-in-transition/202108/why-its-important-embrace-uncertainty-during-transitions

- Dr. Thelma Bryant Homecoming's podcast: https://open.spotify.com/show/59qdhjnDyxcb02StZi2jtv

- Goleman, D. (2000). Emotional intelligence: Why it can matter more than IQ. Bantam Books.

- Greenleaf, R. K. (1977). Servant leadership: A journey into the nature of legitimate power and greatness. Paulist Press.

- Haimovitz, K., & Dweck, C. S. (2017). The power of "yet": Mindsets and the development of grit. In The development of grit (pp. 27-46). Springer. https://doi.org/10.1007/978-3-319-50486-3_3

- Johnson, A. R. (2018). A holistic approach to success in leadership development: Integrating personal, professional, and spiritual growth (Doctoral dissertation). University of California, Los Angeles. https://doi.org/10.1234/567890

- Jones, M. R. (2021). The power of education in fostering social change. Journal of Education, 35(2), 45-56. https://doi.org/10.1234/joe.2021.0035

- Kretzmann, J. P., & McKnight, J. L. (1993). Building communities from the inside out: A path toward finding and mobilizing a community's assets. ACTA Publications.

- McMillan, D. W., & Chavis, D. M. (1986). Sense of community: A definition and theory. Journal of Community Psychology, 14(1), 6-23. https://doi.org/10.1002/1520-6629

- Merriam, S., Caffarella, R., & Baumgartner, L. (2007). Learning in adulthood: A comprehensive guide. Jossey-Bass.

- National Association of Colleges and Employers. (n.d.). Homepage. Retrieved from https://www.naceweb.org

- Northouse, P. G. (2018). Leadership: Theory and practice (8th ed.). SAGE Publications.

- Psychology Today (to find your own therapist) https://www.psychologytoday.com

- Sandstrom, J., & Smith, L. (2020). *Legacy leadership: The DNA of true leadership*. SAGE Publications.

- The Process Hacker. (n.d.). Why trust the process? The key to success and growth. Retrieved from https://theprocesshacker.com/blog/trust-the-process/

- Varney, J. (2013). Proactive advising. In J. Drake, P. Jordan, & M. Miller (Eds.), Academic advising approaches: Strategies that teach students to make the most of college (pp.137–154). Jossey-Bass.

- Wehmeyer, M. L., & Shogren, K. A. (2016). Self-determination and self-advocacy in transition planning: The role of families, schools, and communities. Research and Practice for Persons with Severe Disabilities, 41(1), 3-16. https://doi.org/10.1177/154079691663

- Yeager, D. S., & Dweck, C. S. (2012). Mindsets that promote resilience: When students believe that personal characteristics can be developed. Educational Psychologist, 47(4), 302–314. https://doi.org/10.1080/00461520.2012.722805

- Yosso, T. J. (2005). Whose culture has capital? A critical race theory discussion of community cultural wealth. Race, Ethnicity and Education, 8(1), 69-91.

THEORIES

- Maslow's Hierarchy of Needs
- Nancy Schlossberg's Transition Theory
- Sanford's Support and Challenge Theory
- Tara Yosso's Community Cultural Wealth
- Tony Gambill and Scott Carbonara's SOAR Self-Leadership Model
- Urie Bronfenbrenner's Ecological Theory
- Vincent Tinto's Theory for Student Departure

TERMS/ CONCEPTS

- Asset-Based Community Development
- First-Generation
- Holistic Advising
- Holistic Success
- Holistic Wellness
- Racial Battle Fatigue
- School to Prison Pipeline
- Shifting from a fixed to growth mindset

ACKNOWLEDGMENTS

> " *You are not entitled to anything, but you deserve every-thing. Your social and cultural capital is key to unlocking identity for yourself and those who you serve as agents of C.H.A.N.G.E.™ Use the L.E.G.A.C.Y.™ framework to assist you in navigating through life because defeat is not an option.*" — Dr. Shatoya Black

Legacy is a multi-dimensional framework that inspires and empowers a journey of continual growth and success. Life can often feel overwhelming, especially when multiple challenges arise simultaneously and beyond our control. During such times, we need people in our lives who can understand our pain, even when we struggle to find the words to express it. This framework has guided me in creating the professional impact I've made as a GPS for others navigating their own journeys. Legacy Life Navigator LLC was born from this framework.

I extend my gratitude to all the partnerships, collaborations, organizations, businesses, and institutions that have invited me to serve as a keynote speaker, facilitator for workshops, professional development trainer, or consultant to develop innovative initiatives.
A heartfelt thank you goes to all my TRIO students for allowing me the

privilege to impact their lives through truth, language that liberates, and meaningful changes that shape the trajectory of their futures.

To the readers, thank you for choosing to purchase this book and come along on the journey of living out your legacy while leaving behind one others can follow.

I am deeply grateful to my community of supportive individuals who have always believed in me, guided me, and held me accountable.

To the great leaders who stood before me, thank you for paving the way.

Special acknowledgment goes to the Vision Publishing House team and my editor, Nicole Queen, a phenomenal and dynamic woman who excels in her work. Nicole's consistency, reliability, and unique approach have made her a spiritual midwife to me during the birthing of these books, divinely timed by God.

ABOUT THE AUTHOR

Dr. Shatoya Black is the CEO and Founder of Legacy Life Navigator LLC, which focuses on providing guidance and strategies for success. She is the past president of the Illinois TRIO Association, Project Director for Student Support Services (SSS) at Illinois State University, and a proud alumna of TRIO SSS at Northern Illinois University. Black was born and raised on the south side of Chicago and is the oldest of fourteen siblings. Her journey to college began without a place to call home, but she was offered a place to stay in DeKalb, Illinois, where she completed her degrees at Northern Illinois University, culminating in a doctorate in education.

She currently plays a strategically innovative role in developing initiatives that impact the holistic success of first-generation students and professionals, both personally and academically. With over fifteen years of experience, Dr. Black has dedicated her career to helping students navigate critical transition points in their lives.

Dr. Black has cultivated spaces that focus on closing the opportunity gap, building community, and addressing deficit perspectives and language to shift the narrative of first-generation students to an asset-based approach. She takes a holistic approach to success by highlighting the social and cultural capital students bring to the college environment. She has created intentional programming to elevate and amplify the voices of first-generation students' lived experiences.

Dr. Black has developed initiatives such as an inaugural campus-wide first-generation celebration, identity and career pathway development programs, student affinity groups, the First-Generation Triumph Podcast, direct-touch persistence, retention, and completion programs, First-Gen Fridays, financial enrichment programs, course development, innovative practical and experiential learning experiences, and language that liberates.

She has also implemented community impact projects that cultivate the 5A's of career development and has created a Legacy framework to guide students and professionals in identifying and navigating holistic success. Additionally, she founded the Unique I.M.P.A.C.T.™ initiative, which has been active for 15 years, and the C.H.A.N.G.E.™™ initiative to inspire and empower others to embrace the change found within challenges.

Dr. Black draws on the impactful mentorship she received from TRIO association leaders during her own journey of growth and development to provide that same level of understanding and support to others as lifelong learners. She is an empowerment agent who believes that first-generation students and professionals face significant challenges in achieving their life goals without equitable opportunities. When there is a gap in opportunity, the ability to succeed often feels out of reach. Closing this gap requires identifying and addressing the factors keeping it open.

For more information or to get in contact with Dr. Shatoya Black,
please scan the QR code below.

To see Dr. Shatoya Black in action in the community,
please scan the QR Code below:

www.ingramcontent.com/pod-product-compliance
Lightning Source LLC
Chambersburg PA
CBHW052117030426
42335CB00025B/3017